your permission slip

TO: MYSELF   DATE: TODAY

your permission slip

TO SELF-ACCEPTANCE, FORGIVENESS, AND LETTING GO WITH GRACE

WRITTEN BY

ALEXA GLAZER

YOUR PERMISSION SLIP
TO SELF-ACCEPTANCE, FORGIVENESS, AND LETTING GO WITH GRACE

ISBN-13: 978-0-578-39845-7

First edition • April 2022

dedication

To my sadness for showing me I'm alive.

table of contents

your permission slip

TO SELF-ACCEPTANCE, FORGIVENESS, AND LETTING GO WITH GRACE

Vulnerable

I stood naked in front of you.
I showed you each scar and shared every wound.
Instead of telling me you didn't know how to care for
me, you closed your eyes, crossed your fingers, and
dug into me deeper as every wound started to bleed.
You broke me. You broke me and sat there watching.

preface

I'm not a poet. In fact, I've never written a poem in my life outside of a haiku in maybe fourth grade English class. But I've always admired the honesty in a poet's words. There's something so special about those who can put letters and words so elegantly together. That when they do, it leaves you feeling something so deeply and so connected to something inside of yourself.

I've always wanted to do this. I've always hoped to do this, but I know that doesn't happen without a lot of bravery and honesty. So to be honest, I had no intention of writing in a way that could possibly, maybe, *actually* leave people feeling so seen, especially from a poem. I wrote "Vulnerable" by accident while I was on a walk one day, a day I spent overthinking and analyzing my every move. Days like this always leave me feeling paralyzed and craving movement and sunshine. Off I went to move, to think, to get some sunshine.

I thought of the countless times I'd heard someone's words, not just in poetry but in music, in books, in movies. When done right, words can make you feel so understood yet at times so very called out. It's your inner self knowing that there is no possible way that someone could have mustered up the combination of their words or their emotions unless they'd truly been through something so gut-wrenching, so inspiring, or anything *in-between*. In that, I've always felt safe and less alone. I hope you will, too, through the words I'll share with you in this book, the ones you're holding in your hands and close to your heart in this exact moment.

The words in that first poem I wrote were a game-changer for me. They were a realization of who I truly am and how I show up on this floating rock in the sky. That poem showed me:

+ How deeply I can love another human but how scary it can be to be loved in return. To be fully seen. To let someone in. I now know this paradox of feelings is normal. It's human.

+ My brokenness, or at least how my insides have been rearranged and sometimes not so gently. How my heartaches and breaks have affected me and the bittersweet feeling that sadness means I'm so fucking alive.

+ The bravery and the vulnerability it takes to give someone a chance, an opportunity to let someone inside your being, and to put yourself out there in the world.

+ Most importantly, it showed me my superpower. That I love fiercely but not without fear. I love even knowing damn well that nothing lasts forever. Knowing that loving another human being is risky but full of so much magic. Knowing that sometimes even temporary is shorter than we expect. My superpower is loving fiercely regardless of the temporary because all that matters is this exact moment in time. So let's slow it down, shall we?

These realizations aren't just mine to be had. If you let yourself, you'll have some too. Some of you may have already. I know it can seem like a lot, but in doing this, I promise a deeper connection to yourself and to others.

I think we're all the same to the core, and I know some people won't like that statement. That's okay. At our core, we each have a heart, a brain, and a vessel that is our body. On the inside, we're all built relatively the same, right? We each can choose love, hate, grief, bravery, resilience, or anything *in-between*.

Of course, there's the obvious. We each look different, we act different, we believe in different things, and overall we experience life way differently. But collectively, I think we focus too much on the things that make us different. I think seeing those differences and acknowledging them are important, I do. But focusing on *only* our differences pushes us far apart from one another. It forces people to put up walls and shut down internally. To judge and perceive without empathy. To communicate in a way that puts people down.

Y'all, we need people. We need connection. We need love. Outside of a heart, a brain, a body, that baseline that we all share is that we're all deeply scared of something. Yes, that something is different. We're all going through massive shit. If you don't think so, please open your eyes wider. Yes, that pile of shit looks different for everyone. You may perceive others' shit to be easier or harder than your own. However, start to work out that empathy muscle of yours because we all get the gift of choice. We can choose to believe that we're each connected or we can choose to keep focusing only on our differences.

I think we can acknowledge our different experiences, privileges, lenses, and traumas while also acknowledging that, at the end of the day, we are all people. We're humans, doing human things, feeling human things, experiencing human things. All of us are just small specks of life on this floating rock in the sky. Small specks of life that are all uniquely necessary. We're all just people going through hard things, beautiful things, and simply just trying to figure shit out as we go. That's what it means to be human, right?

And like I said, I know some people may not agree, but it's on my heart, so I'm choosing bravery and sharing it rather than keeping it inside. Right now, I'm choosing connection. To connect with someone, somewhere, hopefully. Maybe you? Right now, I am trying my damn best to see everyone through the lens of similarity. Through the lens of basic human emotions and needs. What's it hurt to try? Because I really can't think of how any change can happen without us all connecting to each other in some way, without us coming together even at that baseline of simply being humans.

We've never been here before. Of course we don't know what the fuck we're doing. Again, flex that empathy of yours.

I'm here, holding my breath a bit. Having lost hope in the short term and finding hope and myself again in this journey. I'm not healed; that's not a thing. I'm healing and picking up the pieces of my beautiful, shattered glass heart.

This is not just a book of poems but rather a collection of the rawest emotions, words, and stories I've ever experienced. I hope you enjoy them. I hope they tug at your heartstrings. I hope you feel something— that you let yourself feel something. Please take what resonates, hold it in your hand, practice it, try it, love it, and leave the rest behind. You don't have to take it all. That's going to be too heavy. Thanks for being here.

My whole heart,

Lex

To love takes courage.
It takes risking, trusting, and knowing that you will
get hurt at the end of it.
That your heart will break one way or another.
Whether that end comes quickly or takes it's
time, grief always shows up because everything we
experience in life, even the most magical, always end.

Let's be friends

This book is more than just words on pieces of paper bound together to create something you're able to hold in your hands. This book, these words, are my heart speaking its utter truth. This book is written by a version of myself that's crossing her fingers and word vomiting everywhere. (Sorry for the gross visual, but it feels like the truth, my truth.) It's a version of myself that I love so innocently, so sweetly, so proudly, and so deeply.

I hope these moments we're about to share together touch you in the form of hugs or the way the sun kisses your face on a chilly fall day. That gives me the warm and fuzzies inside just thinking about it. You know what I'm talking about, right? The little bit of natural warmth that sends the right amount of energy coursing through your veins. The energy you've been craving, needing, wanting, even just for a moment. The kiss from the sun, the hug from a beating heart, that reminds you that you're alive, even when you may not feel like it. That you have the ability to stop and be present. I hope that's what this book is to you. A reminder, a permission slip, a hug, a push, a safe place for your soul to be, to land.

I hope these stories, these thoughts of mine, challenge you to your core. Not in a scary way but one that helps guide you to being the best version of yourself. The one that can love themselves so innocently, so sweetly, so proudly, and so deeply just like I've been doing these days.

Please know you're allowed to challenge me back. Kindly, please. Connection and conversation are what helps make this world go round. I know I just said we're the same to the core, which I stand by ever so firmly. But our differences, those things that make us unique, are the super glue to growth, love, and connection. They're what help solidify change and movement. I want you to think, but ultimately I want those new thoughts and ideas to help you start feeling something new. Something unknown. Something you've never let yourself feel before. Go after it.

It's easy for us to stay in the comfort of where we are. To stay in what we know. To live a life in which we keep surviving. But what if I told you that there is something beyond just surviving your days? That in taking each experience and emotion for what they are—good, bad, and anything in-between—that you'll no longer just survive, but you'll find yourself falling in love with you, your life, and the people in it every single fucking day. That doesn't mean it gets easy. It means you're going to find the peace you've been unknowingly searching for, that your being has been craving.

My hope is that in this moment—and the moments to come as you continue reading— you feel free to roam your brain. That you go inside each and every crevice, every dip, every hidden spot, and that you allow yourself to believe in your imagination, your wonder, your worth. I hope this book helps you expand your intuition, for you to finally trust it. That it stretches your heart to places filled with an amount of love you didn't even know existed inside you. That it gives you a broader perspective on the human experience, one that makes you feel safe to be you.

If you're new here, welcome. I hope within the next thirty seconds you feel like we can be friends if you don't feel that way already. It's important to me that you feel like it's just the two of us sitting across from each other with our beverages of choice while we talk about life, love, and everything *in-between*. I'm giddy just thinking about it. I'll grab my drink; you go grab yours.

Now that it's just you and me, let's get to it. I write so that I can process what I feel. I write because it's physical proof of where I was, where I am, and where I'm going. However, sometimes knowing that writing something down gives proof to an experience or a feeling is the exact reason I don't want to write it down at all. Can you relate? Because writing it down files away the moment, in the moment. It attaches a unique thumbprint to the memory so that I can't just make up a story one day. Writing it down means I have no secrets. It means I'm turning a moment into history. It's a real treasure to look back and see how far you've come, but it can be a real challenge to get yourself to go deeper into a place you wish you didn't exist at all.

I write first to process. I write second to share it with you and the world in hopes that you'll feel something, anything. To feel whatever it is that comes to the surface. For you to be expansive in your feelings, which means feeling beyond just happy or sad. It's time to strive for more than just happy. It's time to not run away from your sadness, your pain, your anger, and anything *in-between*.

Have I lost you yet? I hope not. Please stay regardless of any temporary discomfort. If you stay, I think both your brain and your heart can go somewhere you haven't quite been yet. It's scary, I know. To go somewhere unfamiliar, especially led by a complete stranger like myself. However, it's so freaking worth it. I pinky promise. We'll get through this together. It's your time to let someone help you, to not do this alone, to not pretend you're okay when and if you're not. I did that for a stretch of time. The rubber band finally snapped. I don't want yours to snap, too.

THE HISTORY OF LIVIN' THE DREAM

Years ago, I wrote a book called *Livin' the Dream...Today Because Tomorrow Is Not Promised.* I wrote that in the midst of what I thought was heavy grief (key word: thought). I'd just experienced the worst year of my life, the year my dad unexpectedly died and an eight-year romantic relationship died, too. I figured it couldn't get much worse than that.

I'm laughing a little internally now. Laughing out of discomfort, because if you're anything like me, you laugh things off anytime you're uncomfortable. I'm someone that wants to make everything fun. Clearly, grief is not fun. So I usually disguise it. I pretend to make things fun by laughing or putting this cheesy smile on my face, which often makes things slightly uncomfortable for anyone I'm with. I laugh when I actually want to cry. I put on that cheesy smile when I'm nervous that what I just shared is going to make someone run off in the other direction.

For the longest time, I didn't show any tears or sorrow because I didn't want anyone to think I was emotional. However, the nervous laugh and the cheesy smile are purely my body regulating emotion or showing up as a defense mechanism. I ignored that for a long while, and I bet you might, too. I no longer ignore my being when it's trying to tell me something.

Anyway, I wrote that first book, I traveled some places, I did some things, and then a worldwide pandemic hit. The start of this pandemic became one of the worst years of my life. If you know what I mean, you know what I mean. That year was an internal battle I wasn't ready for. Or at least, I didn't think I was ready. It felt like World War Three, only the fighting parties were my mind and my heart, my grief and my love. Fighting this war has been the ultimate test.

The thing about living during a worldwide pandemic that I find cool—and cool totally is not the right word, but maybe it'll ease the heaviness a bit, which is something I think we need at times. The "cool" thing is that during this time, we're collectively living in a world where every single person is grieving. It gives me chills, actually. We've all always been grieving, just no one knew it. No one was ready for it. No one wanted to go there. How dare we talk about and feel things so taboo to society. This grief has always been here; it was just underneath a lot of "stuff." The reason this is good, the reason it's "cool" is because no one can possibly feel alone in their grief anymore. No one should feel like they have to hide anymore, although I know this will take time.

We're all more aware of our grieving; it would be nice if we could get on the same page about grief and actually talk about it. That's a dream I'll continue dreaming. If no one else will talk about it, I will. I'll start the trend and hope y'all follow my lead.

MY STORY IS NOT YOUR STORY

Things are about to get spicy. The type of spicy that makes your nose run, your forehead a little sweaty, your eyes a little watery. I'm saying this to ease some of the heaviness. Your nose might run, your forehead might get a little sweaty, and your eyes might water a little while reading this book, not just from the spicy but because of the honesty. In fact, I hope that happens. I want you to feel and to push through any discomfort. Don't worry; I'm already feeling all of the discomfort while writing and I'm only a couple pages in. I'm right there with you.

I know why we don't talk about grief openly. It's tough to feel and even tougher to find the language to put it into words. Let's just rip off some band aids.

I thought I wrote an entire book about my grieving process after my dad died. I thought I had it all figured out. In my first book, I wrote about this exact topic. Grief. The thing is—if I am being honest with myself and with you right now, which I promised myself I was going to do—I now realize I may have made that grieving process look some type of way.

To some readers, I may have made the grieving process seem easy enough. Of course, we all see what we want to see. We perceive what we want to perceive both internally and externally. We each get to decide how deep inside someone's story we'd like to go. After that decision is made, people get to think what they want. I've heard it both ways. I've had people share with me that they couldn't believe what I had gone through and also people telling me I had it easy, or that I'm still just lucky. So I'm just gonna shoot it straight from here on out. I'm not going to sugar coat anything, and I'm still aware you will perceive as you choose.

Please remember, this is *my* life story. It's coming from my perspective, my learnings, my feelings. You can take what resonates and leave behind what doesn't along the way. I am by no means perfect, and neither are you. Nobody is. I'm just a human. Trying. Trying really fucking hard. So are you. So is everyone. Let's recognize that together.

What I've come to understand is that I made a super traumatic experience of mine look and feel a certain way for myself. That involved me running off to beautiful adventures to hide and push away the dark demons showing up internally. I did this not because I wanted people to think it was easy but because I didn't allow or want myself to go near some of these hard feelings. Who actually does? I wasn't ready to process and didn't even know how to process them if I tried.

This traumatic experience I'm talking about was me losing my dad eight years ago and the rough year that followed. Sure, I let myself feel some hard feelings for about a week, but then I went back to the million distractions I had in my life. School, dance, work, friends, and my first serious boyfriend. My life may have looked a certain way to people because I wanted to believe that I could smile again during a time when I truly felt like I never would. I wanted to believe in that smile so badly because my world literally felt like it was ending. Maybe you can resonate with that right now, and if not, sadly you'll probably understand that feeling one day.

Eight years ago, I chose to smile. I chose that instead of being fucking sad. Was it right? I don't know. I don't really believe in right or wrong. In fact, I'm trying to not have to always be on one side of the spectrum. To have to make a point to agree or disagree. To be a yes or a no. To feel good or bad. I'm trying to be somewhere *in-between* for once. To be a maybe. To live in the gray. To lighten up a bit.

What I do know is that me smiling and chasing happy was all I had capacity for at that moment. Instead of feeling the melting pot of emotions caused by life in general—the good, the bad, the ugly, the beautiful, and everything *in-between*—I not only wanted to give myself hope, but I wanted to give y'all hope, too. Hope that it could get better. That it will get better. That the shit each and every one of us goes through has to get better.

The truth is that it does get better. Now, I smile and mean it. I also cry my fucking eyes out pretty frequently. I no longer feel like I have the capacity to only feel one thing: happiness. It took years of me subconsciously running away to a year of traveling full-time while living in a van solo, to a very sudden feeling of overwhelm, stuckness, and complete lack of control from a pandemic, for me to finally slow down to a jog. To eventually rest and completely stop the chase. To stop the pursuit of happiness.

I wrote that first book so you could feel less alone in your grief, and I'm still writing for the same fucking reason. The difference is the connection I now have to that grief and the purpose of it. It's much deeper now. I hope you want to evolve with me. That you're okay getting deeper into your feelings and experiences. I want you to feel less alone but not just in your grief. To feel what it truly feels like to be alive in today's world. A gentle reminder that your sadness and entire spectrum of feelings is proof that you are alive. I promise I'll share more on that later.

That first book of mine damn near felt like my baby. If I happened to be in a room filled with people who were saying how many kids they had I said I had "one." That's how much I felt like that book was my baby. Just like any first-time mom doesn't know what they're doing but 'moms' anyway, many first-time writers also don't know what they're doing but just write anyway, learning through mistakes and mishaps along the way. That book was what I *thought* my legacy was made of. What I imagined people talking about when I left this side of life. What I hoped people would attach my name to. I thought it was pure gold and the magic you (and I) needed to live out the dream. But now?

Well, now I'm here. A new person in a new space of existence. I have many new thoughts to share, some that may contradict my old thoughts. That's evolution, baby. If you did read my first book, something I wrote that I can still get behind is sharing "that life is just a series of contradictions." So although I feel like I'm contradicting some of those old thoughts, I'm still in full alignment with a lot of ideas that are deep in my core. Since I wrote that first book, my heart has been split, cracked, and broken wide open once again. Rather than wishing it to be different, I'm choosing to let it be proof that I'm living my life.

I'd like to think that my first book was me being "strong" Alexa. I had armor on for myself, my family, and you. Rather than trying to prove to myself that I could have grace and compassion for my grief, I was trying to prove to everyone else that I could be okay. And, not just okay one day but okay as quickly as possible. Sure, I shared my strength in dealing with something really fucking hard. However, I wasn't actually doing the hard thing. I wasn't actually showing real strength because now I think strength comes through vulnerability. Sharing what's really on our hearts. Feeling what's really going on in our bodies. This book is not about wearing that armor; it's about taking it off and showing you everything that's underneath.

The first book was me unknowingly seeking approval, the approval I thought I needed, maybe even deep down wanted. However, this book is me really just trying to seek approval from myself. For me to be okay being me, Alexa Freaking Glazer in all her glory. I want you to be okay being you. This book is me trying to walk into the world naked. Not actually naked, of course, but the feeling of it, of being without my armor. The feeling that people are seeing all of me. The feeling that I can't hide anything. That feeling can be liberating once you actually feel comfortable with yourself to walk that walk.

It's not just you feeling good in your naked skin but to feel comfortable with that skeleton underneath. The heart of yours that holds everything from your past, present, and future. It's the comfort where you're finally not seeking approval, validation, or instant gratification. Instead, it's about having confidence within yourself.

So here I am, naked, alone, and vulnerable.

Now that I just made it weird, I'm so glad you're here with me. I'm grateful that you're giving me the space to share my stories and that you're taking the time to actually read them. You have no idea how much it means to me. It's been years of pretending, of moving through life wanting to be something I wasn't or not feeling understood in who I was. I finally got really tired. Or at least tired enough. I got tired of explaining myself, my actions—or lack of actions. I got tired of carrying the heaviness that I wouldn't let surface previously. And I got tired of the pain and grief that would eventually become my partner in crime.

I published that first book back in 2018 and didn't record my audiobook until 2020. I did so during that pandemic I mentioned having the joys of living in (still living in at the time of writing). Recording that audiobook was the wakeup call I didn't know I needed and one I didn't know I should've been more prepared for. It was in those moments, reading the sentences of my first book, sitting in the closet of my parents' bedroom, that I realized I was not necessarily ready for the healing journey about to happen but that I had no choice. I got emotionally, mentally, and physically exhausted real fucking quick, but I decided I had to push through. I made it through with a lot of grace, a lot of breaks, some space, and a lot of hugs, which are hard to come by in a pandemic where you need to stay six feet apart from people.

I was done and this is why. I no longer wanted to tell everyone why I wrote my first book. It rolled off the tongue too easily and felt too robotic. Watching people get uncomfortable with that response made me cringe. The pity from them came like a slap in the face. I repeatedly had to say the words, "I started writing as a coping mechanism when my dad died unexpectedly." Instant pity followed, usually with a template response that people give when they hear something tragic. "Oh my gosh, I'm so sorry for your loss." Barf.

Now, I don't blame anyone for this response because I've said it to people many, many times. Just like no one talks about grief, no one talks about how lame of a response it is. Can we come up with something a little more original? It's 2022, people. Not only did I get sick of repeatedly telling people that my dad died because, well, that sucks. I don't need the constant reminder because I live it every day. But I also got really sick of society's shit. The surface level responses, the lack of empathy, and overall people not actually knowing the value or the meaning of the words they're using. I got sick of their perfectly templated apologies and responses.

The *I'm sorrys* I received didn't make me feel better. They made me feel pitied and disconnected. I felt alone and pretty instantly judged. I always felt that people just felt bad for me. Which again, I get, but I just wanted people to want to get deeper. To have a conversation with me rather than run away. To not be afraid of my grief. I think that was what made me so scared of it. I was scared because I felt like I should be based on everyone else's responses and reactions to grief.

When I received those "I'm sorry for your loss. How can I help?" responses, my own responses became lame. Most people—myself included—respond with something like, "It's okay, no worries!" I hate that, and I know it'll take ages for us to collectively stop doing this, but I can't help wishing it were different. I hate that we have to think something is okay when it's not. I hate that we say sorry when we don't mean it. When we didn't do anything. I hate that we have to pretend to be strong, to be afraid of grief just so others can feel more comfortable.

Clearly I started to feel a lot of resentment toward the way we quickly react to things. The way we get small. The way we try to fit in. The way we all put others before ourselves. Aren't you tired? I sure as hell am. How much longer are we going to keep running on fumes? Eventually we'll pass out. I hope you take this seriously. That you notice your words matter. Your growth matters. Your thoughtfulness, or thoughtlessness, matters.

Before working on this book, I thought I was ready to write a story about winning grief. As if you can even do that. I thought I would be writing a book of accomplishment and that writing it would be easier and fluffier than it was. Honestly, it destroyed me for a bit. I told myself, "I wrote my first book because of death. I'm writing this book because of life." Instead, I was pretending to be alive for years. I was just surviving like I told you to try not to. I didn't realize that writing this book, getting closer to a breakthrough, an awakening, would cause me to take radical responsibility for myself, my actions, and my heart. This book is something *in-between*.

When I made the decision to stop running and to start feeling, I realized what being alive is actually about. It's not the fake smiles, the pretend happiness. It's not the mentally tough people, the disciplined. It's allowing yourself to feel everything within the human experience. To have a strong vocabulary you use to describe the feelings happening in your well-equipped body. Although some of it is fucking painful, I promise you that you can handle it. Your body is tough. You are tough. Within your vulnerability, of course. Not just your armor. Yes, sometimes it gets really fucking foggy, but the fog will clear and the sun will hit your face like that gentle hug once again.

My own fogginess made me cringe. I wasn't truly living, and that made me sad first, disappointed second, a million other emotions to follow. I didn't feel alive in my body, and I still wrote a 400-page book essentially on how to live the dream, which everyone translated into "aliveness." Back then, I simply wasn't ready for that aliveness. I was ready to try out my independence and to claim my life in very slow strides.

Now, I'm ready to fully claim, fully test, practice, and live my beautiful fucking life with all of its wild unknowns. To actually be in the space that I like to call *the in-between*. To others, this space may be an awakening, becoming, the healing, or whatever other phrase you would like to say that helps mold you into the best version of you yet. Ladies and gentlemen, I have arrived.

This in-between has taught me how to understand (or attempt to) not just the world I'm living in but myself. The body that is the vessel to my being. It's in these chapters that I found myself honoring the in-between deeply. I am the best version of me and not because I am happy but because I let myself be whatever I am on any given day. I am the best version of me because I work on finding pure peace and presence and because I chase my curiosity like I am running from the freaking cops. Right now, I'm sharing what I've uncovered about the human experience, the lack of empathy the world has for our hearts, the way society has conditioned us, and our deepest desires as human beings.

In a world where many of us focus on the filters, fakes, people pleasing, toxicity, heartbreak, lies, trauma, and grief, in a world where you feel like you want to be anyone but you sometimes, we'll focus on love instead. You're safe to be *you* here. Please (I'm actually begging you) be fucking you here. If and when you ever feel like you can't be you, come back. Come back to right now. Here. All of your feelings are welcome, all of you are welcome here.

Let's get you out of your head and into your heart. You + me friend. You + me.

November 13, 2020

I remember asking myself what am I going to write in this next book? Everything bad has already happened. Truth is, I didn't face any of it. I ran for the last seven years trying to "find myself" and "live life to the fullest" when part of living life to the fullest means living everything. I was doing it one sided. I was living the happy, the cloud nine moments, and anytime something lesser of the good happened, I avoided it. I cried but quickly moved on because that is what society says to do. To be tough, to be strong. The shit that society needs to figure out is that being tough and being strong is actually feeling everything that makes you want to stay in bed all day. To be vulnerable … that's fucking strength.

December 21, 2020

Here's an unpopular opinion: I am thankful for 2020 and the mad pain it's caused my heart. I'm thankful because it's taught me to stop running, to love what is right in front of me, to challenge my own thinking, to sit in so much unnerving discomfort I've wanted to scream, to unlearn the stories I've made up about my past and relearn how to act in the present. I'm thankful, maybe you should be too? Thankful doesn't mean happy, don't get it twisted. Don't put words in my mouth that just because I am thankful means that I am happy that this all happened, because at times I'm not. We're all human. But I'm a believer it all happens for a reason no matter how happy or unhappy that reason makes me. I have to say though, find a couple things that did make you happy, that were good and hold them tighter to your heart. Remind yourself that just like the bad happened for a reason, so did the good things that are happening in your beautifully, chaotic, perfectly imperfect life.

LIFE IS JUST A SERIES OF CONTRADICTIONS:

Rules are made to be broken
Get comfortable with being uncomfortable
Secure and safe isn't always secure and safe
Being selfish isn't always selfish
Perfect your creativity
Be perfectly imperfect
The only consistency in life is change

Never too much, Always enough
You're not too much stop telling yourself that
The right people in your life will want you exactly how you are
Those people will understand your emotional baggage
The skeletons in your closet
The rocky past, confusing present, and dreamy future
The right people won't try to change you because
they will love you just the way you are

your permission slip

The weight of what I want to share with you is riding on my shoulders. It's heavy, but I think I'm finally strong enough to do so. To no longer let it weigh me down but to lift it up and off. I'm feeling the magnitude of it all. The magnitude of my life, my experiences—both wonderful and terrible—and the feelings I'm finally allowing myself to feel and see.

The thought of doing this feels icky. It feels like I have something stuck in my throat. My palms are sweaty. My heart is beating fast. My blood pressure is rising. I have tears flooding my eyes already. My thoughts are moving a mile a minute, and I have chills all over my body. Sexy, right? I told you things would get spicy around here. However, if you're anything like me, I do think vulnerability is sexy, and in this moment, I am going to ride that out.

I'm going to get real here. I think you've been able to recognize that from the previous two sections. I'm not just going to get real in these next couple of paragraphs or pages as I tell you how freaking terrified I am for you to read this book. Of course, I'm stoked for you to do so, but dang, putting yourself out there for the whole world to make their own judgments of your heart is quite the risk. I'm proud of how brave I am for doing so, but that doesn't mean this is easy (like I hoped it would be). This book is going to be the realest I have ever been up to this point. I'm pulling back the curtain. I'm baring my soul. I'm taking away the filters, the societal standards, the conditioning. This is me. I'm real, I'm unlearning, and I'm taking up some serious space with no apologies attached.

You know when you were a kid and you had an imaginary friend? This friend felt just as real to you as any other human in your life, but nobody else could see this friend of yours. Some pretended to for a while, some rolled their eyes at the existence of this imaginary friend, some wondered when you would get over this phase, and maybe even eventually some told you your friend wasn't real. As you grew up, the imaginary friend showed up less and less for you, and you eventually came to know that this friend was all in your head. However, that imaginary friend, although not a real person in the physical, helped you get through life. This imaginary friend was with you when you were scared, lonely, and sad. You eventually learned from this friend that you could count on yourself.

There came a point in my adult life that I became my own imaginary friend. I know this may seem weird, but it's people like me who learn this when they want to be okay being alone. When they want to learn how to enjoy their own personal company. I had a version of an old me antagonizing the new me. I had a version of me that would hype me up when I felt down, and I had a version of me that quickly grabbed any lesser-than-great feelings and hid them before I even noticed they were there. These imaginary friends of mine got me through some tough times. I love and appreciate them for it. I acknowledge their existence but have given the control back to the present version of myself. The one I think is a total badass. The one that doesn't need to ask all these older versions of me for help but purely listens and lets my intuition to guide me to figure things out for myself.

The funny yet not so funny thing is that I thought I was always showing up as the real, current version of who I was. I thought I was already sharing so deeply with others and myself, but I was wrong. I'm here now, allowing myself to show up in a way that feels hard, big, and scary. I'm asking you to read these pages with your own lens of curiosity, a fuck ton of empathy, and an open heart. I'm asking you to allow yourself to think big and to feel even bigger. I want you to move through this book with me. To take note of my language and open your mind to the language you use. I want you to know you're not alone, that you matter, and that you're freaking enough.

I've felt really called to share this chapter specifically with you, but to be honest, I'm struggling with finding the correct words. I'm struggling to put all my thoughts to paper in a way that you can hold in your hand and close to your heart. In a way that you can digest.

I want this book to help you move through life knowing you do, in fact, have someone who has your back. That you have someone to help you with this really hard shit we never asked for but have to deal with. I know I'm just a stranger to you, but sometimes that's all it takes. Someone that's walked the walk. Someone who is willing to tell you their stories of falling in love and getting their heart broken, of making mistakes and fucking up, of celebrating cloud nine moments and any and all other unimaginable places their heart has been. I'm willing to do that for you. I'm ready to break through this internal resistance of mine and talk to you with my heart split open.

I didn't get here alone though, that's for sure. If I did, I probably wouldn't be sharing the things I'm about to share with you. Therapy has been a driving force behind why I'm willing and able to share this with you.

Doing things alone and being alone was always my safety net. Maybe you've felt this way, too. This safety net made me believe in the idea that when you're alone, you can't hurt people, disappoint anyone, or lose those that matter to you (yourself included). What a crock of shit. The truth is that's simply not true. Period. It's no way to live life. More on this later, but truly we can't and shouldn't try to do this by ourselves.

This narrative of being alone was the boost I tried to give to my ego. My ego wanted to protect me; that's what it does. It protects us from our outer world, but if we're not careful, our ego can really put a damper on things. That over-protection caused me personally to be unbalanced and to lose control of my desires. To not focus on what I actually wanted which hardened my heart and emotions. I lost sight of what's important to me.

Deep in my heart, I knew I didn't actually want to do this all alone. I only shared these thoughts with the people that made me feel safe in doing so—and trust me, that doesn't mean that I haven't gotten some tough love. I very much have. Some tough love from the people I love. Although it hasn't been easy, I'm grateful. I've needed the push to share these stories to the degree that I do truly want to share them. Because honestly, I'm so scared and normally, I feel like I'm pretty open to sharing.

I'm scared to share my wounds with you because they're the type of wounds you can't physically see, and what I've learned is that many people judge not only what they can see but also what they can't. It's easy for us to say we don't care what people think of us, and I will continue to aim toward that daily, but it's a pretty human thing to be nervous about what others are chattering about behind your back. At times, it feels impossible (which is a word I don't even believe in) to show up bravely. But fuck that noise. I'm going to try anyway.

Ultimately, I'm not scared you're going to hate me, although the pushback I received after my last book does make me worry that someone will take something I say out of context. However, I'm not doing this for them. I'm doing this for me, and then you. Specifically the one who this is going to impact deeply below their surface. So, yes I'm a bit scared that you won't like what I have to say. That you won't like the person I show up as today. Now, hate is a rather strong word and a word I rarely use because of its strength. So the fact that I am using it at this moment is proof it's just on my heart and the thing currently keeping me up at night.

I know better than anyone that this is a lot of pressure to put on myself. Don't you think? I can't make up your mind for you. I can't control what you think about this book or me for that matter. I can only control myself writing it and the fear that isn't going to stop me. So, I'm just going to let you be the judge (internally dying inside). I know you will be regardless of me asking you to or not.

Many of us—myself included—put this same pressure on ourselves because we know we can't help other people's perception and judgment of us. Because of that, we all put so much fucking pressure on ourselves to do the right thing, be the perfect person, and to not disappoint a soul along the way. News flash—to you and definitely to me—there's no such thing as the right thing. There is no such thing as the perfect person, and of course we're going to disappoint people along the way. That's life, babe. However, the disappointment is on them, not us.

That being said, this pressure stems from the fact that I don't want to disappoint you, the reader, my new friend. Next, there's my dad. I didn't want to disappoint him because my entire first book was about him, his legacy, and the things I learned from him unexpectedly dying. Then, I didn't want to disappoint my mom, sisters, family, and friends who I care deeply about. I soon concluded that being afraid to disappoint people was no longer a good excuse. I wanted to do the right thing by you and by the people in that circle. Who doesn't want to do that, right? But the right thing is just doing the thing in true authenticity. It's staying true to you and not letting your fears win.

Last, there was a piece of myself that wanted to keep my armor on. It started to get cozy in there. I wanted to continue to be the person that sat high on her pedestal, the girl who could go through really hard shit and still smile. And yes, I do go through hard shit and still smile, but there's way more to me than just smiles.

I still hope I don't disappoint you; that's in my nature. However, through the tough love from my circle, the conversations I've had with myself, and my deep desire for you not to feel alone in the hard stuff you're going through, I realized I ultimately don't want to disappoint *me*, myself, and I. Selfish? Maybe that's what it sounds like to you, but to me it sounds like "about fucking time, Alexa." I don't want this book to be finished with missing sentences, paragraphs, and chapters. I don't want to leave half stories. I know leaving shit out would be easy, and it would feel less scary, but ultimately it would really disappoint me (again) and eventually that would be harder to deal with. I can't do it anymore.

Every single time we worry about everyone else, we lose a piece of ourselves that's really important to our story and our existence. We stray so far away that we get lost. It's time to come back home. Home to our bodies, our minds, our souls, spirits, and hearts.

It was in a season of tough love that I was reminded why I'm writing this book to begin with. A quick answer to that is because I literally just want to help one fucking person. Now, I know a lot of people say that shit and don't actually mean it. But it's true. One person is the goal, and I have to be okay with the fact that I personally could be that one person this book changes and no one else (doubtful, though, if you keep an open mind). It's a risk I'm willing to take because without risk, there is no magic. If it's not just meant for me, maybe it's you? That would be freaking awesome.

GETTING BELOW THE SURFACE

We hear this question a lot: "What's your why?" Can we start to go a bit deeper though? I'm sick of the surface level bull shit. I want us to connect deeply, and I say that to you after just telling you how terrifying it is, but hang with me. I'm willing to take the risk if you will. If we go below the surface, below the simplicity that is your 'why,' I like to ask myself:

- What's your why?
- What in your life provoked you to do this or want this?
- Why the fuck does it even matter?

Well, my why is to make people feel seen, heard, and loved. What provoked me? Oh boy, the many times I've felt misunderstood. Alone. Not seen, not heard, not loved. Because of this, I even felt a lot unlovable. I felt that love wasn't meant for me, by me, or from anyone else. I couldn't understand how my heart could love others so deeply, so fiercely and yet I could surround myself with humans who took from me without a care in the world. At the time, I wasn't aware that love is me; truly it is, and what a beautiful feeling that is. That love is always present. That love is hands down my most favorite fucking thing about myself. That love in all of its form is the literal air I breathe by the second. I'm not unlovable, and neither are you.

Let's take it a step further. Why does that matter? Why does it matter that I want people to feel different? Because constantly feeling like you have to prove yourself to people is exhausting. I don't want you to be tired anymore. Because feeling alone seems so bonkers to me living in a world full of 7.53 billion people.

I have to think that someone out there has to fucking care. I have to think that there's no way we're actually alone or should possibly continue to go through life without someone understanding us. That in those 7.53 billion people, there are our soul mates, our friends, our people. That the people meant to stay and show you your life's purpose are the people who are willing to take the time to look at you in a way that you feel understood and to talk to you in a way that makes your defensiveness melt. To be able to stand powerfully in a room without someone being offended by how you show up or you needing to explain who it is you are.

Let's take it one step further. Getting a little more below the surface—which is my favorite thing to do. This matters to me because I want you to see you, hear you, and love you first. For you to feel so strongly about your being. For you to be so confident in the imprint you're leaving. For you to actually enjoy the fact that people notice your perfectly imperfect impressions that you're marking your relationships and the world with. That's why it matters.

That all sounds like gravy (sounds good), but this book isn't all about butterflies and rainbows. It's not a book on how to live your dream, how to stop grieving, or how to love or get over heartbreak. It's simply a book with stories, with lessons, with thoughts, feelings, and with everything *in-between.*

My first book was a book of lessons I learned from my dad. To this day, it holds such a special place in my heart and also in many of yours. This second book, though? It holds *my* lessons. It also holds a special place in my heart and hopefully yours soon too.

This book will share how I've navigated what it really means to live not "the" dream but "my" dream. How I have allowed myself to actually grieve. How I've moved and grooved life with a ton of heartbreak and still have found love—inside of myself. And I hope that maybe you can take something from these lessons and apply them to your own life.

I'm sorry if you bought this book solely as a pick-me-up, a motivational speech, or simply a part two of livin' the dream. You're going to have to be a little bit more open minded about some things. About moving through feelings and not around them. Maybe that seems like a bit much, but I'm going to share with you how I did this. I'm not going to lead you into a dark room by yourself. I'm here, and I hope you know it's safe.

Here is your permission slip. Signed, sealed, and delivered to you. I grant you permission to claim yourself. The permission slip you don't actually need but think you do to feel everything. Your humanness needs to feel your emotions. Your humanness is waiting to be seen. Your humanness has been born ready. Are you?

I mean it though. I want you to feel your sadness, your anger, your happiness, your peace, and once again, *everything in-between.* This is your permission slip to grieve, to heal, to share, to love, to be you. The permission to change your mind, to listen to your gut, and to evolve.

Your evolution will happen regardless. It's the natural progression and development we have as humans. However, to change is to modify. It's the act of becoming. This change takes intention. Allow yourself to get behind that intention and leave things behind.

Here's your freaking permission slip to end the stigma and go to therapy. I'm not going to sit here and say we all 'need' it because that feels like a major call out. However, I do know we all can take something away from therapy. Something more than we expect to. Something beautiful. It's time to put your mental health first. To unlearn everything society has taught you and to relearn what you want, what you need, what makes you and only you feel better.

Together, let's cry in public, stay in on a Friday night, not get out of bed when we're depressed, and live life however our soul and spirit are connected to do so. Go on, stop apologizing for things you didn't do, for being happy, or for being sad. It's time for you to grant yourself this permission unapologetically. Right here, right now, claim your wants, needs, and great desires.

I can't wait to see what you come up with.

June 8, 2021

Vulnerability isn't a weakness. It's a freaking strength, and there is nothing more attractive than someone who is willing to be vulnerable. Tell people when you need a hug or to be held. Cry your eyes out in public if that's when it comes. Don't hide it. Get a little awkward; that's human. Have the hard conversations; they're necessary. Tell secrets (only your own) and share moments with people. Life is too short to keep that guard up forever. Let it down, friend. You'll be braver because of it.

July 2, 2021

You're not too much. Stop telling yourself that. The right people, the right person, they want ALL of you. The right person will understand the emotional baggage you carry, the rocky past you had, the confusing present you're in and the dreamy future that's waiting. They will wipe away the random tears, love on the insecurities, and tell you about the crumbs on your face after eating. The right person will never think you are too much because they will think you are just the right amount of everything.

livin' the dream ...

I used to be known as the "livin' the dream girl." I spoke about livin' the dream on stages. I wrote about it in my last book. I created a movement called Livin' the dream ... THE MOVEMENT. I talked about it all over social media daily. I held up signs everywhere I traveled with that saying written on it. I even have a tattoo across my arm that says it. I lived this identity through and through, and I felt like I was experiencing my dream while keeping my dad's dream and his legacy alive.

If you didn't read the first book, the saying "livin' the dream" was my dad's mantra. He said it, lived it, and believed in it wholeheartedly. It wasn't some end all be all, or glitz and glam; he preached it because it was his every single day. When he left, I wanted to keep that mantra singing. In fact, what I created then was everything I thought I wanted.

I still wholeheartedly believe in that dream, in what I created "livin' the dream" to be, to stand for. But my mind is shifting. My thoughts are expanding. My heart is exploding with new information. Information that makes me feel a little squirmy sometimes because it's me challenging me. It's challenging how I processed my thoughts back then versus how I process them now.

Something in that shift makes me feel like I'm betraying my dad, my family, and everyone who has supported me and my "livin' the dream" ventures, which is many. I know deep down I'm not "betraying" anyone, but because it was all I talked about for years, it makes me feel like an impostor. I know many of you are probably saying, "What would your dad say if he were here? He would be so proud of you regardless." And sure, I bet he would be, but we're playing with "what if" conversations at this point.

Writing down my new ways of thinking makes me feel like I'm getting ready to disappoint people (maybe even you, but I surely hope not). This is probably why it took such a long time to write this book after the last one. In the last chapter, I gave you permission to change your mind. Well, that was me giving myself permission to do the same. The permission to step into my own, to have a voice and use it.

I think it's safe to say that there are a lot of systems in today's society that are broken. Systems that make it really hard for people to move through life confidently, openly, and willingly. I don't think how I built or shared mine and my dad's idea of "livin' the dream" is broken, but I think it deserves some re-evaluating. Some reframing. Some more depth. It's important to know that at times, we have no choice but to operate and to function in society's not-so-great, sometimes fucking terrible systems while we juggle finding our own balance, our own hopes for change, our own beliefs, and advocacies.

It's a real privilege for me to sit here and not just write these words but have someone edit them, have them turned into a book, and then finally have them read by you. Sadly, it's taken me a long time to realize what a privilege it actually is. I've been naïve; I've had my eyes closed. I'm in a space where even though I'm dealing with something that is emotionally, mentally, and financially draining, I *am* dealing with it. I am able to deal with it. I understand that that's not the case for everyone.

I understand that there is an *in-between*, not just in our feelings but in life as a whole. That my ideas, my thoughts, or my life hacks aren't going to look the same for everyone because of these broken systems we grew up in and continue to be part of. Even my newest, most intentional of ideas are going to be a real challenge for some no matter what. I hate that for the world, and I'll try my absolute best to continue to evaluate and fix any of my personal systems that may be off or broken. Not to mention, I will do my damn hardest to challenge other, larger systems that are off or broken, and I'm continually educating myself on what's happening outside of "my" world. We get stuck in our world and our own personal problems a lot. Truly, there is not a 'one size fits all' approach to life, and we all experience everything uniquely.

I know I just said that we're all the same at a baseline. That's still true. Did you know 99.9% of our DNA is the same? We are only different from each other, on a scientific, genetic level, by 0.1%. Now, I'm no scientist, and I definitely do not base all my life decisions off science, but I think if we started to look at that 99.9%, we could start fixing some of the bullshit and the broken systems. We could see that everyone needs certain needs to be met. We could see that, even with that 0.1% difference, we're all just people trying to survive and thrive. What if we approached these changes with one thing and one thing only: love? Too woo for you? I don't care. I truly think that we could fix every problem if we acted out of love, with love, in love.

Now that I went on a bit of a tangent, my hope is that as you read this, as you listen to me change my mind and expand on my ideas, you simply take what resonates and leave behind what doesn't. That you keep an open mind and are willing to try some new, hard things, but that you don't use this book as some end all, be all checklist or bible to live your wild and crazy dreams. Simply do your best and I'll do mine.

I am sitting here right now holding on to the fact and realizing that it's not about working harder all the time. Which many of us are taught. It's not about doing more to the point that you're just filling up your day for shits and giggles. It's about being better, being more intentional, and being aware of how you are showing up in the world. That's what it's all about.

If you spend all your time working hard, making money, creating a legacy, and the million other things on your to do list, you'll never actually experience much. If you think about it, the amount of things we have to do and could do is literally infinite. We could all write to-do lists that go on for days. Throw away the damn to-do list! (And this is coming from someone who loves her lists.)

Before I tell you what I think livin' the dream is—because it's a very thought-out answer at this point—I want you to consider what "livin' the dream" means to you. Ask yourself:

- What does "livin' the dream" look like?
- What does "livin' the dream" feel like?
- Do I actually want that?
- Am I currently "livin' the dream?"

Remember, there's no right or wrong answer. I'm curious though. When you hear someone say they're "livin' the dream," do you think they actually mean it or that they're being sarcastic? I know I've seen it both ways. Sometimes people are honest and really believe it and love the life they are currently living or working toward. However, sometimes people respond super sarcastically and are actually hating (or just surviving) most of the things that consume their life.

Next, I'd like you to consider the American Dream. (If you're not familiar with the American Dream, hang tight, I'll dive into that in a second.) Again, please remember there is no right or wrong answer, I don't believe in that shit. Do you think there is a difference between just livin' the dream and living the American Dream?

Now that you've thought about it, let's talk about it because I'd like to get you behind the idea that they're two different things. One is completely based on your own decisions and desires and one is a perfectly templated idea of what life should look like for those of us who grew up in America.

In my very personal opinion—and I think the opinion of many of you—we grow up thinking we have to want and live up to the idea that the American Dream is the holy grail. It's delivered to us in the form of a checklist of "shoulds" from a very young age, and if you stray away, you'll have many people questioning the way you live your life. A boatload of judgment is usually attached to those questions. This judgment comes from the idea that you aren't checking things off quickly enough, or maybe you aren't checking them off at all. To me, this idea of a dream is a standard that we just shouldn't need to uphold anymore. It's called growth, baby. Not everyone wants the same thing. Let us live, America.

The pressure of this is bullshit. The list of "shoulds" typically looks like this:

- Go to college
- Find your person
- Get the degree
- Commit to that person you found
- Get the next degree
- Find a good ass job
- Marry that person (even if you don't really see yourself happily ever after with them)
- Work, work, work
- Have the most adorable kids
- Save and invest your money
- Be safe, secure, and comfortable.
- Vacation once a year
- Live for the freaking weekend
- Be on the *pursuit of happiness*

Does this resonate? Many of us have been taught that this is what life should look like.

For me personally, when I sit and think about that life—the American Dream—it often makes me feel behind. Like I'm doing something wrong, that I am weird for wanting something else. I'm thirty years old (twenty-nine as I am typing this). I did not go back to school for a Master's Degree. I am not married and not close, although I'd love to be. I chose not to marry my high school sweetheart because although that would have been a cute story to tell, I wouldn't be happy right now. My marriage would not have been what I hoped for and especially not what I dream of having in this moment. But because of that, because I chose to do life alone for a while, kids really aren't in sight either. However, my biological clock is ticking, and I have the world constantly reminding me that it is.

Furthermore, I didn't decide to go into corporate America because although it would be nice to have a stable paycheck and health insurance, I chose a different path instead. I chose to live in a van and travel the country. I chose to work in the restaurant business for a long time because I didn't want to commit to only two weeks off the entire year. I chose to do the scary thing and do anything but stable as I tried to make my passions a career.

If you want pieces of that dream—to go to college, get married, have kids, have that stable paycheck—that's okay. That's one million percent your decision, and it may be what livin' the dream looks like to you. And that's cool! Maybe it's not either of those scenarios, and that's okay too. Fuck yes if you're confident in that and fuck yes if you decide to go after whatever it is that you desire.

My point is that you get to decide. You *should* decide. No one else.

I get it. Going against what we're told is best for us is scary. It's really scary to want to do something different. To do something that maybe hasn't been done before from our perspective or that of our nearest and dearest. It's hard to get yourself to color outside the lines and go against the grain. I challenge you to want more for yourself. More as in do the thing you actually want to do, whatever that looks like to you.

~~LIVIN' THE DREAM~~ LIVIN' *YOUR* DREAM

I think living your life in this way—the *livin' your dream* way—is the opposite of having a checklist. It's not an end all be all. It's a daily practice. It's allowing your unique human experience to unfold and combine it with your deepest desires. I swear they can all be possible. This type of life is about deciding what you need—not just want—in your life to feel human and to feel alive. It's choosing *you* over everything. And that, my friends, is much harder than we'd all like to admit.

My idea of the holy grail is not a list of shouldas, wouldas, couldas. It's a list of doing shit on your terms, fucking up, celebrating, learning, and growing. When we decide to live life like this, we grow in unimaginable ways. Because when we're not learning, we're not growing. When we're not growing, we're dying. This type of life is about creating the things you wish existed—big or small. It's not answering to anyone else but yourself. To check in with your heart constantly.

I mentioned a little bit of what my personal life looked like. How I made some decisions on my own instead of following a checklist. But I still did some of the things on that checklist. I still went to college, have some of my money hoarded away in an investment account, and very much want to get married to the person that I am madly in love with and have a family with them one day. I also embraced a period of travel while living in my van. I didn't go back for graduate school, and I made some other 'unconventional' decisions. That's me livin' *my* dream; now you get to decide what that looks like for you.

Here are some other examples that may suit you. Instead of going to college or grad school, you may realize you can learn a lot from things like Google or YouTube. Maybe you want to go to trade school instead. You may decide it's more important to you to find yourself first and "your person" second. It could be about doing something you love regardless of the financial security or health insurance you get or don't get. This may look like getting married to your dreams and desires before or ever standing up at an altar and looking someone else in the eyes. Maybe it's deciding that you don't want kids. That you'd like to invest in yourself, or an idea, or a business venture instead of hoarding your money into some untouchable account.

Ultimately, me preaching this is all about putting your life in your hands and your hands only. It's you being in alignment with yourself.

THE EVOLUTION OF "THE DREAM"

When I talked about livin' the dream in my first book, I believed that this lifestyle consisted of five things: sacrifice, the grind, humility, small victories, and happiness. To me, it highlighted the ups and downs. It was proof that livin' the dream wasn't just for the rich and famous, that glitz and glam, and that thing you get just when you have a lot of money. This version of livin' the dream explained that you still had to go through shit in order to live a life like this. It wasn't going to be all butterflies and rainbows.

I still believe in this, I do. I just think there's more to it. I think I missed a couple of things, and if I am really honest, I don't like the fact that it ended with happiness. To me, that pushes people on the pursuit of happiness track as being the end all be all. However, I'd really like to push you to the pursuit of peace instead.

I never wanted livin' the dream to be something that looked easy and ended with a big shiny bow of happiness at the end because the truth is that nothing really changes when you have it all. Life still gets hard. Emotions still come up. That stuff doesn't just stop when you've reached some idea of how you hoped to live life. Livin' the dream is not a band aid for all of the stuff we don't want to deal with. I think that's why some people use this phrase sarcastically. Because they do think people that "look" (again we're perceiving here) like they are livin' the dream don't go through hard things anymore. They do, trust me.

If I look at those five things I mentioned earlier—sacrifice, the grind, humility, small victories, and happiness—I now see more. On a deeper level, I see that sacrifice will look different for all of us. The grind will look very different for each of us. Showing up with our gut checks and being humble will change from person to person. Small victories will be everything on the spectrum, and happiness, at times, can be a real bitch to feel. That end goal can even feel unattainable when you're in the thick of some heartbreak.

I wish back then I had added curiosity, empathy, and peace to the list of things I felt were important in order to live the dream. I didn't then, but I do now. Curiosity is the desire to learn. This is valuable to you because showing up with curiosity is being not necessarily ready but willing to learn about yourself, your traumas, your soul. It's being open to learning about others without trying to change them or save them. It's being open to learning about the world and not shut things down just because you didn't see it in the past. Curiosity allows you to change your mind. Curiosity allows you to be who you are and gives the opportunity for others to be who they are. Curiosity makes you fucking better day in and day out. Fun fact: if I could describe myself in one word, this would be mine.

Next, empathy. The way you can allow yourself to be curious is by having empathy. Empathy is holding space for one another regardless of not understanding what someone else may be going through. Empathy must show up more. You must give time for your empathy muscle to get stronger.

Last, you must find peace. Peace in the in-between. The pursuit of peace is accepting the fact that you may be feeling multiple things at once. That you're experiencing so many things at once. This is the main thing I know now. If we focus the dream on being happy all the time, we will surely be disappointed. If we focus on having peace, we will have way less disappointment, and honestly probably a lot more happiness anyway.

Now, if I look at my original pillars of sacrifice, the grind, humility, small victories and happiness through the lens of curiosity, empathy, and peace, I think we can actually attain our individual dreams. Your dream has no timeline, and this is not about counting on other people or other systems, it's about truly believing in you, counting on you.

Sacrifice is the need to either give up something or lose something in our lives. To understand that sometimes sacrifice chooses us and other times we choose it. What I mean by sacrifice choosing us is when we lose something not by choice. Maybe that is similar to my case like losing my dad. Maybe it's you getting laid off from a job, or maybe it's the fact that collectively there are 7.53 billion people living during a worldwide pandemic. Collectively, in those experiences, we didn't get a choice.

Then there's the sacrifice that you chose. Owning a business, staying in on a Friday night regardless of your FOMO (fear of missing out), or exiting a relationship that is no longer serving you. How is this part of the livin' some kind of dream? Sacrifice is a teacher. A teacher that proves that no one actually knows what they're doing, that we simply just need to do. Sacrifice teaches you what's important and how to manage yourself through hard times.

The grind is to thrive under all conditions. To do things when you don't want to, when you don't see the light quite yet at the end of the tunnel but you take strides toward it anyway. I look at motherhood as a grind. My sister Nikki and her wife Mindy recently had triplets. Yes, triplets and all boys (they are so freaking cute, I can't believe I am just bringing them up now). They also have a three-year-old (he's my favorite but shhh, I know I'm not allowed to have favorites). The mothering doesn't stop. The need to feed and change them doesn't end. I imagine that it's very hard for them at times to see the light at the end of this tunnel. When will they ever have a normal sleeping schedule again? When can they go somewhere without having four car seats in the car? But this family is part of their dream. It may look a little different than they anticipated, but they are in love with their family and ultimately their dream of building one. Raising legends has become a priority to Nikki and Mindy, and that doesn't come without a boat load of sacrifice in the midst of it. But they "mom" anyway.

Next, we have humility, which to me is the gut checks of life. It's knowing that no one is safe from hurt, heartbreak, and the reality of being a human on this planet. It's acceptance without entitlement. Humility is a quality that makes you get all the warm and fuzzies. It looks a lot like celebrating some successes in silence. It's celebrating others regardless of where you're at. It's saying thank you and doing without expecting anything in return. It's actively listening and not always needing to chime in with your experiences.

Small victories are up next. These are the small pockets of joy in your day that remind you to be grateful for the good, the bad, and the ugly. It's moments of hope that remind you that you're doing the best you freaking can. These small pockets of joy remove you from the spiraling about getting stuck in twenty minutes of traffic. Picture this: you get stuck in traffic, you're twenty minutes late to work, and you're now frustrated and annoyed. That typically gets carried throughout your day. I know because I have road rage at times and strongly dislike getting stuck in traffic. Before you know it, a bad twenty minutes can turn into a bad day, then a bad week before you recognize it. If you don't care about traffic, think about the last time you had a bad day. Was it a bad day or a bad five minutes that you decided to milk all day? If I (and you) took the time to celebrate the small victories, those tiny pockets of joy during the day most likely I would never spiral about something so insignificant.

Last, please don't make this "the life goal" or the ticket to livin' the dream. We've got happiness. In my first book, I described happiness as an everyday choice. I said it's as contagious as the chicken pox, a lifelong pursuit, and that just like wine, it gets better with age. Again, I don't think any of this is wrong, but I don't want you to think that happiness should be the end all be all. If we look at happiness through the lens of curiosity, empathy, and peace, we will know that we need to feel everything else in order to feel true happiness. Yep, that means bring on the sadness and everything *in-between*.

Livin' the dream isn't easy for anyone; however, it may be more tangible for some. We need to connect more deeply with ourselves and others to lift each other up from love to live out our wildest dreams. It's time to get in our feels, don't set this book down just buckle up.

July 1, 2020

I remember being so starry for a full-time life on the road. Thinking I was going to be off the grid, hidden away in the mountains or on a beach somewhere and that things would be seemingly wonderful. But this life, it's all one giant contradiction. I am the same human, in the same body, but shit, I am such a different human in the same sense. I have a bigger heart and wiser mind, a lighter touch and a stronger hug, a tougher immune system, a more open ear, and such a high craving for curiosity in this world. I struggled the most yet was also the happiest. I had very little money but was so rich in experiences. You have people who think it's the most epic lifestyle and others that look down on it and don't care to understand.

I remember thinking I would be alone at all times but was surrounded endlessly by people. I never stopped being challenged, sometimes by choice and other times by the universe. I've never been more creative and also so stagnant in my life. You see, everything surfaces when you live life so simply. Your awareness is heightened, and it aims at becoming your best friend or your worst enemy. I have felt so close to my dreams and also the biggest failure of my life.

This to me, the contradictions, the cloud nine moments and the rock bottoms, that's the dream. Livin' the dream doesn't mean that life is easy it actually means life is really freaking hard but you do it anyway. It's humbling yourself through boundless expectations and living such a messy and beautiful disaster. I wouldn't trade this for anything. I wouldn't trade it for my wildest dreams to happen right now in this exact moment because deep down I know they will happen. I know this because this life has taught me that the universe will show up when it needs to show up and that we're all going to be okay.

December 20, 2021

Remember, just because someone shares openly and vulnerably does not mean that they aren't scared to do so. They just decided that choosing bravery and connection was more important to them. You can too.

LESSONS ON LIVIN' THE DREAM ...

Sacrifice | the need to either give up something or lose something in our lives

The Grind | to thrive under all conditions

Humility | how we react compassionately to the gut checks of life

Small Victories | small pockets of joy and winks from the universe

Happiness | the choice we make to have the warm and fuzzies

Curiosity | the desire to learn

Empathy | the ability to hold space for another human being

Peace | being accepting of one's feelings, thoughts, and human experiences

SIGNS YOU'RE MOST LIKELY AN EMPATH:

You feel deeply for others

Your intuition is strong

You need a lot of alone time

You can not resist caring for others

You can feel when someone's intentions aren't genuine

You take on the energy of others

You feel connected to Mama World and experience healing outside

Exhaustion
I'm tired.
I've been busy holding my breath.

the in-between

The human experience is an experience to say the least. It can be funky. It can be beautiful. It can be happy, sad, and everything *in-between*. There are no rules to how you play and live this gift of life that you've been given. The more you bluff, though, and the more you pretend to simply just exist, the more you'll get sucked deeper and deeper into a less fulfilling life. One you wish you could escape from. One you wish you could trade for someone else's.

But, my friend, if you break the habit of bluffing and pretending, if you start to play this game with true personal alignment and intentional curiosity, you'll begin to realize that life is all about living in the in-between. That it's anything but black and white, yes or no, to agree or disagree. That there is this gray area that is filled to the brim with an infinite amount of wonder and peace. I'd love it if you got cozy there. Cozy in the gray, the maybe, the gap, the *in-between*.

I'd like to think we find this in-between when it's time to be challenged. We may not think we're ready, but the universe knows it's time, and it's our job to trust that invisible knowing. It arrives—never beautifully packaged— when we're ready to test and trade what has been for what's to come.

The in-between is the space in which you question what you've learned and begin to establish what it is that you want to share both with others and with yourself. Oftentimes, this space gives you the sense that you're on the outside looking in. That you're looking at yourself through a lens, a window, another perspective. It becomes a moment in time where you can see two scenarios playing out. One scenario seems comfortable and one seems possible yet a tad unfamiliar.

The comfortable place is where you've been, what you've done, and what you've been taught to do based on things like societal standards, family traditions, or personal patterns. The possible yet unfamiliar side of the in-between is the curiosity to see what will happen if you just allow change to have a place in your life.

If you allow yourself to slowly move from one side to the other, you can always have a place to come back to. To know that your safe place to land can always be the in-between when you're feeling too overwhelmed, too stressed, too heavy, too paralyzed.

At times, you may feel stuck or unmoving in this in-between, but please remember you still have ground to roam here. There are times you may not know what direction you're going, what's left from right, but that's okay. That's where this sweet adventure lies. Yes, sometimes you get lost and have to ask for help. That's okay.

It could feel like too much. It has for me at times, but I've gripped tightly on the knowing that I'm safe being me. Sometimes that lens, that window, that new perspective attaches to an awareness we feel like we're not quite ready for. To see, to feel, to know what both others and ourselves are doing or not doing. Having this awareness may feel like a complete loss of identity or a personal crisis. Been there, done that, probably will be there again.

If this frightens you, I'd like to change your mind, because I'd really love for you to feel the peace and gratitude that is possible if you just befriend the unfamiliar for a little length of time. You always have the choice to move. You always have the choice to say no. You always have the choice to go backward if you so please. I warmly invite you to sit in the temporary unsettling feeling that is this space of confusing but intoxicating wonder.

So although at times you may feel stuck in the in-between, what if we reframe that so you feel like although you're in one space, you have the ability to move and roam in it? That you actually aren't stuck at all. That you are brave enough to see what's hidden behind the doors, in the corners, and in the dark or light spaces that appear in the in-between.

When you enter, it's important to do so with the utmost respect for yourself and the grace from within that will allow you to keep stride. There aren't expectations here. Expectations only cause you to avoid. You don't have to go fast or be productive here. You're allowed and able to move slowly. In fact, you should embrace a slow, slow burn. It's here that you can take your time, think more clearly, and take breaks as needed.

If you're anything like me, you drink too much coffee. I drink too much because I don't spend the time savoring the first cup that hits my lips in the morning. I swallow it whole and serve myself up another mug and this goes on repeat all day (and all night).

Think about what it would be like if you took the time to savor that cup of coffee or enjoy your favorite glass of wine or whatever your drink of choice is. If you were the savory type of person, you would drink it slowly and gratefully. You would do so just like you take your time in bed on a Sunday morning, staying snuggled in the mounds of pillows and blankets that surround you. This isn't being stuck; it's roaming life with presence and an attention to detail. You are not stuck unless you choose to be. Savor the moments and hold on to them like gold.

When you're straddling this imaginary line of what was, what is, and what will be I challenge you to pause. To stay in this space, to stand, sit, and cuddle with the discomfort of the unknown. Of the presence you now have. If you do so, I think you'll like the outcome … eventually.

I think you'll be able to truly walk into the world, into your world, living your personal yet most desirable days.

CHASING SUNSETS AND STARS

The in-between holds a very special place in my life and my soul. If you stay a while, if you allow that pause, you'll notice it has a knack for wild presence and pure fucking magic. It's in this space that you must try your best to feel anything and everything under the sun. To let everything (and I mean everything) come to the surface.

I know this is scary because it sure as shit was for me. I was used to being on one side, the familiar side. To be downright good at the bluff and living in the comfort of my very own patterns. The patterns that kept me running quickly away from anything but happy. The patterns that kept me going toward fun, wild, and provoked my childlike visions. So when I ask you to feel the unsettling feeling of being somewhere in the middle for a bit, I'm only doing so because I know you can even if you don't feel like you can. I know it can feel like an endless pit (it has for me at times) but it's necessary for your growth and your overall energy.

For me, the in-between is similar to watching a sunset, which just so happens to be one of my favorite things to do on the planet…or I guess not on the planet, but somewhere out there, in the universe. Chasing sunsets is where I can forget what's happening "out there" and focus on the things happening "in here." Inside of me. Chasing the sun, as I like to call it, allows me to shut off and enjoy the special moments and to sit in peace, especially if I'm struggling internally. This time is spent acknowledging the wind on my face, the colors in the sky, the smells in the air, the feelings in my body, the noises that surround me. Where can you go to be present in your in-between?

I think a lot of times we don't even realize we have a space that is so closely tied to our own version of the in-between and that we can go there for clarity and truth at a moment's notice. A place and a moment where we volunteer our time to our thoughts and our feelings. Where we volunteer our soul to something much bigger than ourselves.

Think about it. We're just a small speck of life floating on a giant rock in outer space. Every now and again, it's key to acknowledge that. It's humbling and wise to acknowledge that. To know that our beings are small but uniquely necessary. That we are tiny, so freaking tiny. Yet, somehow, when struck with the pain of suffering, we think that our problems should stop the world from revolving. We think the world should pause, open its arms, and come to our rescue.

Friend, the world can't pause for us. It's *your* job to slow down time. The world is always opening its arms to you; you've just not been present to that fact. The world won't rescue you, but you sure can rescue yourself.

You are always able, if willing, to sit fully in your body. And although tiny in the scheme of this galaxy that we get to soar through, you get to be mighty in your ability to be okay with being small and being human. To live another day, to roam through your human experience. To do more than just exist. To enjoy and play. This, right here, is the path to loving yourself and your life so much that you're no longer willing to go even one more day without an insane amount of intention. This is the art of having your own back regardless of how icky floating through space may get at times.

When I lived in my van traveling around the country, I began to notice my attraction to sunsets and began to prioritize them throughout my days. I would wake up at the butt crack of dawn in order to be done with my day by the time the sun would settle and the sky would turn into stardust. There's something really magical about watching Mama World go to sleep, about watching the blue turn to darkness, to twinkling balls of fire in the sky.

I did this dance almost daily for a year, and I fell in love with the magic of cotton candy and sherbet-colored skies. I began to understand that this was the gift of the in-between. These were moments in time where the noise of the world was on mute and the volume of my mind was loud and clear. Each sunset was me leveling up to the love that I hoped to feel.

You have access to that same gift; you just have to find the entry point to your in-between.

HAPPY PHOTOS IN A SAD GENERATION

We live in a society that's firing at us from all angles. We're work horses, consuming the world and people through our fingertips by the minute. We're told to keep going, to stop crying, to be better, and that although perfection doesn't exist, we should at least be striving for it. It may feel uncomfortable to be existing in this. And it is so hard to take in that much information.

However, I'd like to argue that it's also hard to simply exist without true awareness in the world today. Without awareness, we have no connection. I noticed this when I truly began connecting with people on a deeper level. The more I connected, the more I watched people release their secrets to me. I listened to their problems, their big emotions, and their complaints. I watched these people turn into humans right in front of me. However, these folks continued to bluff to the rest of the world and ultimately to themselves.

Right now, we live in a sad generation filled with happy pictures. We find prompts daily that tell us to "post a video of a time when no one knew how depressed you were …" and typically that video is the person looking like they were having the time of their life. We see pictures of all the relationship and career #goals while rarely seeing the struggle it took for someone to get there or their day-to-day struggles.

This ambiguity has the tendency to make us feel really freaking alone, and it makes it really difficult to show the realness of what it's like to be human today, or really just human at all.

So, rather than cheering other people on; admiring them for pushing through their version of hard, messy, and unknown; or finding true connection through shared experiences; we decide to project that their life experience must be created from overnight success or maybe they just figured it out and I can't. News flash, no one has it figured out! This thought alone becomes painful really fucking quick. It causes each one of us to attach to some serious impostor syndrome.

Of course, I get it. I think we project this certain idea of an emotionless, easy life as a sense of hope that maybe, just maybe it actually could be happy, perfect, and easy for us, too. But in doing this, we unknowingly discredit our own human experience and that of others. We miss connection all together because we keep putting ourselves and people in bubble after bubble. We keep thinking that we're doing life wrong and everyone else is somehow doing it right. But how could we? How could we possibly do something like life right? We've never done this before. No one has. Collectively, we're all experiencing this for the first time, and I don't know about you, but I didn't get an instruction manual at birth.

So the messages keep getting lost. Truth is, we're all struggling. It's life; how can we not? We all have shit going on. We're all going through really difficult things whether or not you see them on the internet. Whether or not someone decides to share this piece of their life with you.

We all experience this difficulty at a different level. There is a spectrum of "hard" that we each have that no one else can see. I'd like to gently remind you that your version of hard is not the same as someone else's. Just because you're dealing with one thing doesn't mean someone else isn't dealing with their own thing. It's easy for us to focus on our world, our life, our problems and to place them in the center of the universe. I don't fault you, I do it too every now and again.

But that's not actually how it works. We each are the center of our own universe, not *the* universe. We're each dealing with things that feel bigger than us even if it is something relatively small. But we're not each other, which means we can't possibly know the internal battle anyone else is facing. How dare we say our own human experience is better or worse than someone else's. We haven't a clue.

We all get in bad moods regardless of how positive we are. We all get envious, tired, sad, want to hermit and shut out the world, or are scared of something at some point. However, we're not living in a sad generation just because we're all dealing with "sad" and hard things. We're living in a sad generation because no one wants to share their sadness with others. That is actually the sad part. Read that again, please.

It's easy to blame technology—Photoshop, TikTok, Instagram, and so forth. They encourage "perfect" moments. But we do what we see. We do what we are taught. Many families (at least in western culture) have never been emotionally open. Each and every generation has their very own ways of shutting down these imperfect moments… and ours just happens to be able to be projected on a larger scale because almost everyone has access to the internet. That's the key difference, right? The amount of presence we all have now is far different than it was before the internet.

The internet doesn't have to be a bad place, though. There is influence everywhere. Some of that influence is helpful; some isn't. You have to do your due diligence and make the decision for yourself on what's helping you and what's affecting you negatively.

I struggle with this for a couple of reasons; I struggle because I've been there. I've posted that exact video of a time I was depressed but looked anything but depressed. In fact, that video is still from one of the coolest days of my life. It was one of my favorite experiences to date, but I was deeply struggling internally.

I was at the RiSE lantern festival in the Mojave Desert with my roommate and one of my very good friends, Mikey. If you've seen the Disney movie Tangled, you know how magical a lantern festival looks, and in real life, it's only magnified. I have chills just thinking about it. I was in the desert drinking vodka lemonades, listening to live music, and writing letters to myself and my dad on what felt like life sized lanterns that would eventually float away into the sky.

The moment couldn't have been more perfect. It was such an intentional time surrounded by thousands of people who were using this day as a way to slow down and consider their gratitude for life lived, life now, and for what life could be. It was truly beautiful.

When I think about the video I shared, I look happy as all get out, and that's what I wanted people to think. That's what *I* wanted to think. Looking back, I ask myself, "Was I faking it? Was I pretending to be happy so people thought I was a 'stable' human being? So *I* thought I was a stable human being?" Fuck yeah I was. Being depressed sucks, and I didn't want people to pity me. I didn't want to pity me.

I've mentioned a bit about empathy, and I think the cure for that pity we can feel (which is actually what sympathy is) is empathy. Empathy is one of my number one values. It's saying "shit, that's hard." It's holding space. It's connecting and listening. At this point in my life I knew what empathy was, and I could practice it for others. However, I wasn't aware of a thing I now like to call "self-empathy." I wasn't having any consideration for my own feelings. So just as I would try to feel for someone who is going through something painful, I needed to do the same for myself. I needed to stop being disconnected from my body and practice that empathy within.

I'm no longer willing to put a fake smile on to "seem" any certain way for people. I invite you in your own time to do the same. If you're not ready, I understand. I'm not going to pretend it isn't an adjustment or that it's not scary. It's also really hard not to subscribe to the 'happy photos in a sad generation' notion unfolding in front of your eyes. It's hard to be who you are, to let your sadness flag fly. To be willing to be vulnerable. To share that sadness with others. I hope you're ready soon.

I want to put something into perspective for those of you who are like me and tend to be really hard on themselves when they aren't productive or happy. If you're reading this, chances are very high that you're living in a worldwide pandemic or were around for it. We will eventually get through this, but the world is forever changed. That being said, that is sad. We literally weren't allowed to go outside. We lost people, lost ourselves, and had to get really comfortable with grief. We couldn't hug our family, high five our friends, or shake hands with strangers. That's sad as fuck. Of course we're living in a sad generation. Of course we're feeling wonky and lost in these feelings that we've never allowed ourselves to feel before.

But friends, what a unique situation we are in. A situation where every single person in the world, all 7.53 billion people are grieving something at the exact same time. Some may say that sounds terrible; I think it sounds beautiful. It's beautiful because it's proof that none of us are standing alone in pain. None of us are moving through the in-between alone. There is safety in this, at least for me. We may be physically alone, but check in with your loneliness right now. Check in with your grief. If you are thinking to yourself, "What the heck does check in with your emotions mean?" well, hear me out. Checking in means giving your emotions and feelings a chance to be seen. To truly acknowledge what your body is feeling, what your mind is thinking about, what your heart is yearning for.

When I'm in therapy (I'll share more on when I started therapy and what a game-changer it was for me soon), my therapist always asks me to start the session with my feelings. I sit there, check in, and say, "I feel …" and I repeat that until I either don't feel anything else or can't put any more language to my feelings.

More recently, I've started keeping a "feelings journal," a journal completely dedicated to my daily feelings. I open a page and hash it all out. It's similar to a gratitude list, only I am sitting there being grateful for each and every emotion coursing through my body. I am simply piecing together language because it helps me better understand myself and overall helps me find a lot of relief. I can breathe a little slower and sink into my body a little more. As you identify these feelings and feel them in your own unique way it's comforting knowing that there has to be someone else out there, at least 1 in 7.53 billion, who is in a similar boat to you right now.

I feel like a broken record, but the need for you to feel and then share your sadness (as well as any and all emotions) with yourself first, and eventually with others when you're ready, is a real must. It's necessary for human growth, evolution, and connection. My hope is that we eventually can live not just in a sad generation of happy photos but just a generation of happy, sad, and everything *in-between* type of photos, memories, and experiences.

I want to remind you that this is human. That we don't need to "normalize" anything, we just need to humanize it. To allow our story to unfold. To be present to it and to feel every feeling on the spectrum, that's truly why they exist. Those who are living a life of abundance, freedom, and intention are typically those that stopped pushing away the bad or lesser of the good. Feeling big things, and being aware of those things proves your aliveness. If you look back at my dedication page, it even says, "to my sadness for reminding me I am alive."

Don't forget, it's also human of us to push that away. To not have the capacity to go there. If you're not ready yet, I get it. I wasn't ready for years. Instead, try taking slow, small steps toward the feeling you're trying to avoid. If you don't, they'll catch up to you eventually. They did for me. Twenty-eight years of emotions I didn't let see the light of day and eventually they all came crashing in like a tsunami. Please don't just wipe your tears anymore. Please don't listen to society. Please don't subscribe to just happy pictures. I'm over it. It's not sustainable, and to be frank, it's not healthy.

Please don't shut this book and say, "No thank you, not ready for this." The in-between marks the very fine line between losing your mind and full-on celebration. I know what you're thinking. "Losing my mind, Alexa? No thanks." Stay with me. It may feel unbearable at times, but it's here that you learn the things about yourself that you didn't even know existed. Beautiful, magical things about you. It's here where you begin to show up for yourself and learn your boundaries. This type of awareness marks choice. A choice to continue on the path or change the course.

Here is the opportunity to experience that intoxicating wonder and combine the stillness with the chaos of what was, what is, and what will be. The in-between is a humbling place to be. It allows you and forces you to lock eyes with your truths and brings you closer to what you actually desire in your time here. The place where you can acknowledge your smallness while feeling courageous and mighty as hell. It's okay; stay awhile you might just like it here. In fact, you may just love it here.

November 10, 2020

The world has such a short attention span for things that matter.

May 21, 2021

Sadness is simply your heart talking to you. Talkback, no one likes to be ignored.

WHAT IT FEELS LIKE TO BE ALIVE:

Allowing yourself to feel happy, sad, and everything in-between

Getting uncomfortably close to any and all feelings that you would normally want to run away from

Experiencing all that is the human experience, even when it doesn't feel good

Giving yourself grace and honoring all that you are

In case you didn't realize …
There are 7.53 billion people in the world,
I promise you, someone is going to love you.
Someone is going to care about your story.
Someone is going to understand your being.
Don't be shy.
The world needs you in it.

you are uniquely necessary

Life is just a series of moments. Moments becoming memories. Memories becoming the most beautifully written stories ever told, but only if you decide to actually tell them, to share them openly and vulnerably. To share these stories with the willingness to connect wholeheartedly with yourself and with others.

If you think about it, right now, every second that passes by is changing from present time to a memory. We try to grasp at memories like straws. But the hours, minutes, and seconds that we live fall through our fingers faster than trying to hold fistfuls of sand on the beach. We often think about how much better life would be if we could just freeze time, but we only want to freeze time that treated us "well." What if I told you the key to freezing time, to slowing it down, was to be truly present to it. To not get wrapped up time and time again thinking about how you can save it, hoard it, or trade it. The key is to just use your time while it's here.

We think that the only way to pick up on the details, the smells, tastes, smiles, and delicate moments of life is to remove the noise of pain, opinions, and judgment. However, that pain, those opinions, and the judgment aren't going anywhere just because you hope they'll disappear. The noise simply gets quieter when you spend time connecting with the right people. Connect with the people that build you up rather than put you down.

When we use the excuse that the world is too noisy, we tend to overlook these little moments of life that can bring great peace into our worlds. We need to learn how to focus even with the noise. We need to focus on the fact that those moments of connection, big or small, matter.

Instead, we have a tendency to think that our life story isn't significant because it's filled with insignificant moments. It's us not fulfilling our duty as a human to be present. We believe that our life needs to be 'better' in order for it to carry weight. We believe that our good could always be better. That our bad is so bad that no one wants to hear it and that our in-between is a useless waste of time.

Do you see it? We're always discrediting ourselves, our experiences, and our stories, which leaves us unable to connect with others. Why can't we ever be proud of it all? Proud of how we handled it all? Things are either too exciting or not exciting enough. Just let yourself be somewhere in-between and share that in-between with others because they are probably in the same boat as you. I want more for you—for all of us—but I need you to want more for yourself, too.

It's not about actually freezing time at all. It's about you taking it upon yourself to take a snapshot in your mind, to take note of the beauty of every moment—not just the "good" ones—and being present to them all. The good, the bad, the ugly, and everything in-between. None of this time is useless, and none of your time should feel that way. It's about acknowledging moments before they become just a memory.

No one thinks their story is significant. This stings because I think this is the very thing that connects us to ourselves, our people, our purpose, and to a more abundant life. My hope is that one day we can live in a world where we do find significance in all of the sentences of our story. That we're able to connect with other human beings on another level because we're no longer afraid of ourselves being not enough or too much. It's because of those sentences that you are you. Don't hide it. Publish it.

Now, I totally get it. I went through a very long period of not wanting to tell my story to anyone, much less the world. I didn't want to tell people about my relationships because it made me feel like I was the problem and therefore clearly "not enough" of a person. I didn't want to tell people the story about losing my dad because I felt like people would think I was just trying to get attention, therefore also being "too much" of a person. But keeping those stories locked inside of me made me miss out on the potential to connect with others who had similar stories and who would one day go through similar situations. In hiding my story, I pretended to be someone that wasn't me. I wasn't proud of my story. I resented it.

We forget that every single day we are writing our own epic life story. Every conversation you have, every thought that comes through, every place you go, every experience you have, is you writing new words, sentences, and pages. You're opening and closing chapters of your life as they happen each and every single day. My hope is for you to start piecing things together. For you to start taking those snapshots so you can honor the heck out of your time spent here. To not be closed off to others, to not hide yourself but to finally know and own your story by sharing it with the world. It'll feel electrifying, I promise.

More times than not, we tend to put all our focus on other people. We think the strangers we see plastered all over the internet have a perfect life and struggle with slim to nothing. Because of that, we start to believe in overnight success, perfect relationships, and the ideal life. But is that reality? No, dude, it's not. How can it be?

We so easily forget that every single person on the planet is struggling deeply with something. Remember, we all baseline are the same. A heart, a mind, a body that is a vessel and 99.9% of the exact same DNA. We don't see it clearly because we're so damn focused on wishing we had what we think someone else has.

Not only do we think few people are struggling, but we think that the few that do share their struggles with others must be special. We think they're so brave for talking about it, that they must be stronger than us to not only deal with it but then share it with others. Instead of admiring that, we might decide to feel bad for them, pity them, or maybe even deeply empathize from afar.

What if you could practice that same empathy for yourself? What if you could acknowledge your bravery in sharing your story?

Well, the time is now. It's time for you to own your story and fall in love with it.

HONOR EACH AND EVERY CHAPTER

Imagine there's a book you've been dying to read (maybe even this one, that would be cool). You've pre-ordered it or gone to the actual store to pick it up. You're invested in the excitement around the book, you're interested in the content that's supposed to be in these pages, and you think you may genuinely connect with the author. You open the book and begin reading, but after several chapters go by, you find one has been completely ripped out. You're confused and also slightly annoyed because this book has taken up your time, energy, and money, and now you're left on a cliffhanger. Once you realize one chapter has been ripped out of the book, you rummage through the rest to see if anything else is missing. Other pages are missing, paragraphs have been crossed out, and some sentences are smudged.

Are there chapters or pages you'd like to rip out of your own life story? Are there sentences that you wish were smudged? Paragraphs filled with regret? Words that came from heartbreak, grief, love, and everything *in-between*? My guess is yes. My guess is that you wouldn't want to share a thing or two with some people. My guess is you think your story is insignificant and irrelevant to the world. I get it, I do, but please hear me out.

Just as you were upset about this author leaving things out of their story, leaving things out of your own story should upset you too. I had to wrestle with this myself when I started to write this book. It's in these bits and pieces that you get to share such a special part of you. It's time to give people a little more of you. To give *you* a little more of you.

The easy thing to do is leave this shit out of the story. But when you leave out such a giant part of your story, you tend to leave out the exact parts that made you who you are. That changed you a bit, that molded you into someone new, that stretched you and expanded your view on the human experience in some way.

I have some chapters of my life story I would really love to rip out. Chapters of my story that are heavy, that royally broke me inside, stories so wonderful they feel like a figment of my imagination, and—if you haven't figured it out at this point in the book yet—everything *in-between*. I have the chapter where my dad died. The one where my boyfriend of eight years cheated on me. There's the one I had to have back surgery at the age of twenty-five and had to learn how to walk again. The chapter when I decided to trust a man for nine months over my own intuition. The chapter where I gained twenty-five pounds and hated the body I lived in. The chapter where I lived during a worldwide pandemic. The list of shitty chapters are endless, and if I kept them all from you, you wouldn't be reading a very good book right now. (I hope you think this book is good).

To be honest, I don't think you would even want to read this book if there weren't obstacles and situations I had to overcome. Some resilience I had to build. My guess is that you're probably reading this to begin with because of one of those shittier chapters was the thing that connected you and me. You're most likely reading it because you want to feel less alone (same). I'm here for that shit. Here's the kicker: you and I are not defined by one chapter of our story, and each chapter gives us an opportunity to do what you and I are doing right now, connecting. A-fucking-men friend.

I used to be someone who had some good "Midwest" values. I don't even mean to use that completely past tense; however, some of those values have transformed. I've always been disciplined. However, that discipline was very much the idea to leave my "shit" at the door when I had a mission to fulfill (a.k.a. going to work or being on a team like a dance team in college). I never saw the point in sharing my emotional turmoil with other people because I knew it would just affect the group as a whole, and why should I be the one to bring everyone else down or be annoyed with my complaints or perceived excuses?

I especially felt this way all the way up to my dad dying. My dad died when I was twenty-one years old and dancing at a Division I college. This team was my life, and I put everything I had into showing up to practice every single day leaving my junk at the door. How sad to think my dad dying was just 'junk.' We had a national championship to win, and I couldn't let my teammates down. Well, all of a sudden I realized I couldn't just "shut it off." I realized that I was a different person, and I needed to honor the pain and the differentness, otherwise it would creep back into my life later on (which, of course, it did).

I used to have a friend—key word "had" a friend because this gal no longer is one. More than once, she told me to "not be the girl who lives in a van;" she wanted me to talk about losing my dad because it was a "better" story. Well, I'm not here for a "better" story than the one I got. I want to tell all of the pieces. To leave nothing out. To be my truest, most authentic self so you feel more comfortable being your truest, most authentic self.

First, if you have friends like this, you should really reconsider those relationships. Friends should never tell you to deny yourself of you. Don't let anyone make you feel any type of way about any chapter of your story. They have not lived it. They're an outsider looking in. They don't get to hit publish on your book. You are the author which means you make the decision. Your friends, your circle, and your people should be there to hold your hand, eat way too much ice cream with you when you're sad, and tell people off who are mean to you. Kidding. Kinda …

Let's be clear. I'm not the girl that used to live in her van. I'm not the girl who lost her dad or whatever other bubbles people would like to put me in. All of those moments in time are part of my story. All in which I am grateful and proud to have made it through. They all carry weight. None of those pieces of me are surface level. They're all part of the story that I, as a human, write daily. It's beautiful.

We each have stories that contain some heartbreak. Many times, instead of sharing them, we hold on to them. We hide the grief we carry; we push away any emotions we have. But it's these things that make us special, that makes us so tough yet so soft. These things make our hearts feel empty but in time much, much stronger. It's the thoughts, feelings, and actions that no one knows about, no one sees that fuel us to live better, live harder, to live out our wild dreams. It's us who know how precious life is, and it's us who act on that notion and truly do more than just exist.

January 2, 2020

You want to know why some people lead epic lives? How they manage to come up with an epic life story? It's not because they are more special, it's not because they have more money, it's not because they have better ideas, it's because they take their life story fucking seriously.

February 16, 2020

Friend, you're over here doubting yourself when you have so many others craving your potential. Craving that thing that makes you, you. You can either continue to drown in your negative thoughts or you can evolve and realize, "Damn, I am as freaking awesome as people say I am."

April 8, 2020

Tell that story. Yes, that super embarrassing one or the one you feel isn't that significant. Tell the story of your heart break or your rock bottom moments. Maybe it's the story about having no money, getting your world rocked, or accomplishing something big, like really big. Whatever it is. Tell it. Now. I promise it's going to help someone on their journey.

August 3, 2020

Don't be ashamed of any of the wars you've been in. The many days you fought and fought to try and keep your heart safe. To ultimately keep you safe. Don't be ashamed of fighting for you, your feelings, your thoughts.

December 9, 2021

Every single day we are writing new chapters of our life story. We're making memories and creating stories that can be told for lifetimes to come. However, somehow our brains keep telling us that our specific story is insignificant to the world. So, we go through the motions of life as we're unintentionally writing new words, sentences, and pages. Stories that we don't actually want to be part of. Well, pick up the damn pen and start writing a story, start living your life with awareness and intention. Color outside the lines and scribble your freaking heart out to the point that your knuckles turn white. Fall in love with the good and lesser of it because it's in those moments that you became you. Most importantly, write and live something you actually want to be part of. Your story can be as epic as you want it to be. Don't wait for someone else to write it for you. You are the main character; don't you dare forget that.

HOW TO UNDERSTAND YOUR STORY:

Who do you want to claim to be? Now command the attention you deserve and be proud of who you are. Be that.

It's not all about what you want to do but how you want to feel. How you want others to feel. Do what makes you feel the warm and fuzzies inside and out. Feel that.

Where do you go to create the things that you wish existed? Your happy place, your safe place, the place for innovation. Go there.

What moment in time changed everything for you? Not the moment you knew what to do but that you knew your life would be forever different. Acknowledge it, process it, use it.

Your why is your purpose. Why do you do what you do and why does it even matter? Identify it. Run with it.

Now, that you know some piece of your story own it and go live *your* dream.

The skeleton
I'm just a skeleton.
Guarded by the walls I've put up.
Peaking over them, waiting.
Waiting for what feels like a miracle to cover my
bones and give me life.

grief is not what it seems

Eight years ago, my dad died, and I've pretended to be okay ever since. Sure, I've shared how devastating it is to lose someone. I shared bits and pieces of my heartbreak with the world, but there's so much more to this grief thing than I ever anticipated. I wasn't willing to face some of the things that came up along the way because it made every situation feel like life or death. It made every situation feel heavy, and I didn't feel equipped to handle it many times.

I understood that I would develop some triggers from this grief, but what I didn't realize was that those triggers would show up in places I didn't even imagine. My grief showed up and continues to show up in relationships with men, friends, and family. The biggest thing I became afraid of was the temporariness of relationships that always resulted in me putting my guard up. I didn't realize how much I would attach or detach to and from people and relationships because of my experience with such deep grief (more on this later).

When my dad first passed, I let myself be "kind of" sad publicly. But after a little while, I forced myself to go about my life. I put my armor back on and plastered a big smile on my face. I think a lot of us do this to feel some type of normalcy. My life was one way one minute and completely opposite the next. This is grief. This is change. It's how it works. It throws you off your rocker so much and so quickly.

Looking back, I get why I did it, and I feel so very much for that Alexa who ran away from her grief. I coped this way for a number of reasons. At times, it felt way too hard to deal with. I wanted to give people hope. I wanted to personally feel normal. And deep down, I wanted to give *myself* hope that all of that grief and the feelings underneath would eventually pass. I wanted to believe that I could feel better.

Because of this armor, I never went to a grief group, never walked into therapy, nothing. Honestly? I think I thought I was too good for it. That I didn't *need* it. I was staying positive, I was disciplined, I was motivated, I read the books, I listened to the podcasts, I was writing, I was serving people, and I was going about business per usual. Only my 'per usual' was vastly different because of the change. I was stuck wishing that it wasn't, even though it was massively different. Grief changes everything in seconds, and I became a showcase for continuing on with your life as is.

At the time, I wanted to prove to people more than myself that I could do it. We all attach to something when we grieve in order for us to feel better. My attachment was to the people I felt like I was helping. You're going to grieve however you're going to grieve, but from my experience, it's a hell of a lot harder later on when you do what I did. What I think most do. It's human to not want to feel all the time. But those feelings will promise to show up stronger, meaner, and bigger the more you push them away.

A couple of years ago, I found myself in Southern California where a friend told me about a grief group that was happening at a local coffee shop we hung out at. At this point, I was creeping up on the six year anniversary of my dad's death, and I'd been thinking about my dad often—more often than usual. He would come up so much that I couldn't get it out of my head even if I tried. I felt like I was drowning. This seemed to come in massive waves, so at the time, I was super appreciative of the friend that reached out to tell me about this grief group. I decided to take a chance and go for it even though I was very scared of going. I decided that maybe I didn't need to pretend that anymore. I thought to myself, "Maybe it's normal to need to talk this shit out with people who've walked the walk of grief too."

At the time, I was living and traveling the country in a van. Yes, I was the girl who was "living in the van down by the river." During this time, I remember a lot of people asking me if I was afraid of the loneliness that I might feel being on the road by myself. Honestly, at the time I wasn't (probably my inner voice hyping me up again) because I felt somewhere inside me that loneliness was only for really sad people, and that I wouldn't feel that because I wasn't a really sad person. Eye roll. No shit, Alexa. You weren't sad because you didn't let yourself be sad, which is the actual sad thing.

I also had this idea that I couldn't be lonely if I was surrounded by people. I was wrong. Loneliness is something deep within us and has nothing to do with location, environment, or the amount of people surrounding you. Hindsight twenty-twenty, right? Now I do realize I was lonely in my brain, in my heart, and in my body while I lived in my van. I had a lot of time to think, and at that time, I didn't really know what to do with all of those thoughts. I felt discombobulated, I hated the body I lived in, and I also felt like I should be grateful because I was doing something not many people get to do. Sometimes gratitude can force us to push away the grace we need to have for ourselves in times like this. Be grateful yes, but you're also allowed to feel your shit even if you're lucky, or privileged, or whatever.

The day of my first grief group came, and another friend asked me if I could help her with something in her business that night. Now, the people pleaser in me was like, "Of course I'll do something for you!" The girl that ran away from her pain was also like, "Of course I'll miss the grief group for you!" How convenient. I really did want to go, but ultimately, I was so scared to realize I wasn't actually "okay" and very scared to learn whatever it was I would learn at that group. Clearly, me helping this friend was such a cop out and was an early lesson on boundaries. At the time, I was okay with it. I figured, "I've made it this far without a grief group or therapy. What's a little bit longer without a group session?"

Eventually, night came, and the friend that needed help canceled on me with ten minutes to spare. I remember thinking, "Did this happen so I could go to the grief group? Should I go?" I had a couple of minutes to decide what I wanted to do, and eventually I decided it was best if I went. Cue the stomach drop and some mad courage to get moving.

My van was parked at the beach with a couple of friends, and the coffee shop where the group was meeting was around the corner. I don't totally know what came over me other than the fact it was just time. I knew I needed to go. I literally started to run to the coffee shop and made it just in time. There were a handful of people there sharing so deeply about the loved ones they had lost and the grief they consistently felt.

Today, I am forever grateful that I went, and I'm also a bit bummed it took me so long. It was that night that I shared things about myself that I never let leave my brain prior. The thoughts that made me feel lonely. I felt like I was finally in a space that I didn't have to just put a smile on. Many times before that, I'd thought that my thoughts surrounding my grief were too big, too crazy, and too morbid to share with anyone. I didn't have anyone in my life who would listen and not think this girl is in looney town.

That night, I shared that because my dad died at the young age of forty-nine that I now have an irrational fear of that number. That number has become such a trigger regardless of how I see it or hear it in conversations. For years, I thought my future husband's life would have a deadline and that at age forty-nine, something unexpected would happen. I also realized that anytime someone made it to fifty, I thought, "Wow, be careful, they must have gotten lucky." I intentionally avoided people because I was scared instead of grateful to experience people for any length of time. Truth is, we never know the length of time we or our loved ones will have. I still have this weird relationship with the number, but I'm now able to talk myself through it.

This fear made me detach, and it also made me feel like I was never doing enough because I only had so much time to do it. People always say, "Life's short, don't take it for granted." For a long time, that phrase would make a pit form in my stomach. I'd think, "No shit, it's only forty-nine years long, that's extremely short." What I learned by sharing this fear that night was that other people had a similar fear when it came to numbers involving their loved one's passing.

I also shared how triggering the cell phone can be for me and how I spiral anytime my sister or mom call me or whenever they don't answer their phones. For those of you that may not know, I found out my dad died over the phone because I was living far away from my home town in Las Vegas at the time. It makes it really scary to see "Mom Calling" because my mind instantly takes me to the worst phone call of my life. Telling this story at that grief group helped me realize I wasn't the only one dealing with fears like this.

As I continued to share my demons with others, they shared theirs back. I finally felt a little bit safer in my mind (because my mind was feeling like scary place for a while). I also started to admire the people who didn't take as long to allow themselves to actually grieve. It was at this moment I realized I talked about my dad. I shared stories about my dad, moments in time, but that was it. I didn't share *my* heart. I didn't share my feelings because honestly, I didn't know what I was actually feeling. I realized that if I wanted to heal, I had to grieve, and in order to grieve, I had to share my heart.

Every time we share, we become dependent on how well or how poorly it is going to be received by others. When we share, we take the risk of showing a part of ourselves that we're worried someone will judge us or make us feel less than. Instead, by us sharing, someone might feel more connected to us and possibly think higher of us. That's the beauty of sharing below the surface. When you feel like you want to hide a piece of yourself, eventually that piece of you Is going to want to escape. To be free. When you share yourself with the world, you begin to trust that you actually are perfect just the way you are, and you start building a really strong relationship with yourself. The more risk you take, the more you get a fuller picture of yourself and the choices that you make.

The more I shared, the more I realized what grief actually was and began to accept it. Not simply to accept death but to accept that we grieve, and we grieve for-fucking-ever. If you're unclear, we're not given an owner's manual when we're born to save for later. Grief is an experience—mind, body, and soul. It fills your entire being with every emotion possible. It has no rules, it doesn't discriminate, it's not patient, and it's definitely not linear. We all feel it very differently because we each have this unique grief DNA inside of us.

People tell you your grief will get easier and that in time it won't hurt anymore. I'm sorry to tell you, but it doesn't get easier. It simply gets more manageable. It still hurts. Some days are worse than others, but it's not a constant pain anymore. You do get a little relief, a chance to breathe every now and again. People tell you they're sorry, but why? It's not their fault. It's natural for people to fall victim to giving you sympathy, but what we're looking for is empathy.

Grief changes you, and that's a hard realization to have because it's a change we didn't ask for. Sure, we may come out of this better, and I think if you do the work, you do come out better. However, dealing with that change is still hard. Grief happens suddenly, and we're not initially equipped well enough to handle it. Because grief happens so quickly, it makes everything else in your life carry this newfound importance. This value it didn't have before. You become so aware of how temporary everything is that everything, every decision, every relationship then feels like it matters. The truth is that no one knows what the hell they're doing. No one can know.

My advice for those who are grieving is to do what works for you without shame, without feeling small, and with the utmost courage.

To believe in the fact that you're doing your best and that you're doing it right because there is no perfect way to grieve. It's about trusting yourself to keep going. There is no need to apologize for being sad, for having a day, or for even being happy. For those of you grieving , I hope you find the people who are willing to understand you (or at least try to understand).

For those of you not grieving but know someone who is—or who will one day be walking a similar walk—know that every situation is unique. That each story is unlike any other. Be present and make yourself available. Please remember that even when people stop talking about it, the person grieving never forgets. When the food stops coming and the people leave, they feel their grief—and more alone—than ever. Typically, they want help, but they're scared to ask for it because they don't want to feel like a burden. So please be a friend and open your heart to love them a little harder. Open your ears to listen to them. When they need to feel safe, open your arms to hug them. Have tissues ready when they need to cry and a carton of ice cream ready when they just need a friend.

This piece of my story sucks. I know you have some chapters like that too. I want my dad here more than anything in the world. The reality is though, I am here. I am alive. I can't die mentally, physically, and emotionally just because my dad did. You can't either. Not from any piece of your story where grief decides to show up. When you think you're alone, remember you at least have found a friend in me. You are not defined by your grief. You're defined by your love.

Grief sucks, but the one thing that makes it a little sweeter is that it comes from us feeling an abundance of love. What if we started to thank our grief because it came from us feeling deep love? That love can continue. People love us. Love remains. Love and grief can coexist. Love is inside of you always.

We grieve so deeply because we loved so deeply. We love so deeply because we've grieved so deeply. If we know that forever is always shorter than we expect, then make the choice to love, to grieve, and to experience everything in-between for as hard as possible and for as long as possible so you can be living as big as possible.

May 17, 2021

How do you explain what hurting under the surface feels like?

October 20, 2021

I hate when people say, "What would your dad say?" I would love to fucking know even if it was something I didn't want to hear. I'd love to have those challenging convos with him. Not to get his approval but for him to be proud of what I have become. The woman who makes decisions for herself.

I feel as though I'm betraying him and wanting to challenge him. I'd like to think that he would approve of me being my own person. A human with ideas, and love, and courage, and feelings. I hate the fact that I'll never actually know until I cross over to wherever it is we go. But, right now rather than people telling me what he thinks he would think I just have to stick to my guns and think what I think. Go with what I feel. Because if I don't, I'll keep getting stuck. I'll stay here paralyzed by the questions I had and the unknown of the answers.

WHAT I LEARNED FROM GRIEF:

It always happens suddenly
No one is equipped to handle it but you do it anyway
It's not all bad, you can feel empowered too
Always has you feeling too much or not enough
It's not the same for anyone
You learn empathy over sympathy
It shifts your life in a second
It's not linear
It pops up whenever the hell it wants to
Even happy are sad because they are different now
Time doesn't heal all
Your grief evolves (that doesn't mean it gets easier)
A.k.a. It doesn't get easier, it gets more manageable
No one knows what they're doing
Small decisions can be so fucking hard
Everything holds a newfound importance
It all feels like life or death

Lessons

I hate the fact that some people come into our lives
purely to teach us a lesson
And in that lesson your heartbreaks, your ideas are crushed,
and your hope is lost.

boyfriend #2

From a young age, we start to believe in a certain ideal of what love looks like, how it feels, and how people give and receive it. Many of us learn this from our parents or the people in our lives who we surround ourselves with. As time goes on, we begin to develop a skewed view of love either based on how we grew up or how we begin to perceive the feeling through the internet, movies, our friends, or our families.

We start discrediting ourselves and our truest wants and needs because we think love must look a certain way. We're told by those that love us that it should be a certain way. As time goes on, we feel the weight of insight, grief, disappointment, and our own swarming thoughts, making us question our worth.

If you've experienced love like I have, this weight gets heavy. It gets confusing. It gets exhausting. It's hard to want something so bad and to be so confused about how to attain it in a way that makes sense and in a way that makes you a better *you*. That's what I really want, anyway.

We begin to question whether we're worthy of love, and I think this happens because many of us hadn't learned how important it is to love ourselves first. To look after our own physical, emotional, spiritual, and mental being. I don't think many parents teach us the importance of this, we don't learn it in school because that would be too taboo, and I definitely think society has taught questionable things about love.

Seriously! Think about industries for things like diet and wellness, cosmetic surgery, beauty, and fashion. All of these industries aren't telling us that we're perfect just the way that we are. Instead, they prey on our insecurities to make money, and they are massive. This can leave us feeling empty and like we need to fit in a box, that we need to be something specific in order to love and to be loved.

It's in this that we've learned how to shapeshift. We've learned to change that physical, emotional, spiritual, and mental being of ours that is so uniquely necessary. We take away our superpower of being us in doing this shapeshifting work. If we shapeshift well enough, we don't have to do the incredibly hard work of loving ourselves. Instead, we fit into boxes made by others and at the expense of ourselves so we can maybe, even just for a second, feel love in some capacity. Been there, done that.

Many of us tend to focus on the instant gratification and validation from others to help build us up in the face of love—or the lack of love—in our lives. I don't know about you, but I tend to lock eyes with my heart when it's broken. I feel the void of love deeply when this happens. As if love has completely walked out of my life for good. News flash, people: leave, love doesn't. Love is and can always be present even when the ones we loved walk out of our life.

This realization didn't click for me until the day before I turned this manuscript in (I swear, therapy got me good that day). I know this fact alone doesn't help when you're feeling it so fresh, so raw, or don't believe it at all yet. I think this is what makes us lose hope. If we think love leaves us when people do, how are we supposed to love ourselves when we're alone?

Some people then take it upon themselves to avoid the feeling of love all together because they associate it with heartbreak and pain. Others jump into something quickly to feel the potential of love but never go near the pain or the heartbreak. Do either of these sound like you?

Ultimately, falling into either of those scenarios means you're avoiding the possibilities of love in its deepest form. It means you're forgetting, not aware, or don't feel the love that's right inside of you or an arm's length away. What if love was always—even just a little bit—present inside of you, for you. Could you believe that? I know, it's easier said than done, and it's a lifelong practice. Sit with it. Think about it.

I've done both of those scenarios above. I've jumped into relationships to feel better, and I've avoided them to also feel better. Everything we do is somewhat calculated even when it doesn't seem like it. We innately just want to feel fucking better in the now, so we do just that. We pick the option that will make us feel better quickest with no regard to what that's creating for us later. Hey, it's okay. We all figure it out eventually. At least, we all have the opportunity to figure it out. We typically have a short attention span for our feelings, so we react in a way that makes us feel better and safer, and I fault no one for that. It's human.

In the chapter "Grief Is Not What It Seems," I mentioned that I think we grieve so deeply because we love so deeply and that we love so deeply because we grieve so deeply. Love and grief are one and the same. You may feel better about your grief if you closely attach it to you love like I have. It feels more sacred, more honest, more loving. However, it's in the in-between, the moments where you really sit in your heartbreaks of heartbreaks that you start to understand your patterns. That you start to understand how it is that you love. How you were taught to love. This is when you see and understand what you crave and attract by love, or the idea of love.

In my experience, my in-between came with a newfound awareness. This is where I began to notice who it was that I had loved in my past and how exactly I loved them. This awareness brought up loads and loads of questions. Some questions I'll never have the answer to and other questions that the answers were painful to hear at first. In learning these secrets about myself, I learned I was creating many narratives (that felt so real) in my head. I started to question my wants and needs.

I started to question whether or not I was worthy of the type of love I always thought about. The type of love that I craved deep, deep down. The love I couldn't, at that point, put into words. I began to think that I was either too much or not enough for people. Sometimes both. For a long time, I felt that I was simply just destined for heartbreak after my dad died. It was that grief that has followed me and hidden inside of my heart. It was so deep, it had no air, it couldn't breathe, and it let me avoid yet crave love on each and every level.

In my first book I mentioned Boyfriend Number One, my high school sweetheart, the eight-year relationship, and the man I thought I would marry. I also very quickly mentioned a little bit about Boyfriend Number Two, my head over heels, never too serious, always laughing my ass off, three-year relationship. I then mentioned that I was ready for a much-needed relationship with myself.

The book ended, and I had that somewhat meaningful relationship with myself. It lasted over three years. I thought I was going to learn all this shit about myself (the stuff I'm now just learning), but I was mistaken. That relationship with myself was very surface level. Which is literally the one thing I will never allow in a relationship now. I want all of the below the surface conversations, the vulnerability, the stories that the two of us can muster up.

When I talked about all of the above situations in my previous book, I now realize, looking back, that I was a tad surface level with those things, too. Really, you didn't get much more than I just shared above. That was mostly because I hadn't taken the time to actually pay attention to what had happened in and after those relationships. I wasn't clear on what I'd learned from them yet. I was just sad, angry, and heartbroken. I figured we all get into relationships and the moral of the story is you either get married or break up. Boyfriend Number Two used to always say that to me, and I hated the harsh reality of that statement. However, I now know it's very, very true. Which means you just have to be grateful for the time you do get to spend with someone.

It wasn't until my next serious relationship that I was faced with every single insecurity of my life. I looked at him and basically looked at a mirror of every unsurfaced emotion, thought, and feeling ever. I didn't know that until I was out of it. Truly, when you read about this Situationship (what a fuckery), you'll probably think to yourself "Alexa, it's so clear!" And sure, *now* it is, but when you're in something, you're in something, and it can be hard to see things clearly.

I'm scared to death to write about these experiences. To write about all of these relationships (including the one with myself) because I am scared to relive them. I've already felt myself reliving them by just thinking about what I have to write. To get into my brain and deep into all of these memories filled with every single emotion I have ever felt.

I was scared that I would move backward even though I've been doing the work—with my therapist and with myself—to move forward. I'm scared that the love I finally found for myself will disappear when I remember what I accepted before. I'm afraid that by reliving what society likes to call "failed" relationships, I'll go back to the mantra I used to sing in my head, the one that took up so much brain space rent free: "I'm always too much and never enough." Which I'll let you in on a secret. I did relive it while I wrote this book and went through a two-month depressive episode because of it. I got out of it. It was therapeutic and hard and emotional, but I hope sharing that helps at least one reader.

Ultimately, these relationships hardened my heart big time, and I'm continuously trying to fiercely love on my heart wounds. You know the type. The scars placed so perfectly on the surface of your heart. The wounds that you know how, when, why, and where they came from. Wounds that you know who exactly gave them to you (and maybe still resent them for).

It's about time I openly talked about my heart wounds. I've realized that our body keeps tabs on our heartbreak, on our trauma, on our greatest fears. I first learned about this idea in the book *The Body Keeps the Score: Brain, Mind, and Body in the Healing of Trauma* by Bessel van der Kolk M.D. This book blew my mind and helped me understand how trauma truly stays with us and evolves with us. When struck with opportunity, our body reminds us of the situations and feelings that make us comfortable through familiarity, even if painful. I think in becoming aware of these patterns—becoming aware of our past—we can begin to let grief and love coexist because they're not enemies; they're teammates. They're one and the same, fighting together for love.

I've had a giant wall of resistance up in sharing these stories. I've cried over them time and time again, literally multiple times today as I prepared to write this. In fact, I'm sure people at my local coffee shop are looking at me thinking, "Is this girl okay?" My palms are quite literally sweating right now, and every time I pick them up off the keyboard, my hands shake. I have the biggest frog in my throat, and my teeth are clenched. I'm on the edge of my seat, and I keep taking breaks to take the deepest breaths of life. This is my body keeping tabs on the pain that both love and grief have caused in my life. It's time.

MY HIGH SCHOOL SWEETHEART

As I said earlier, Boyfriend Number One was my high school sweetheart. We started dating in eighth grade at fourteen years old. We were basically babies and quite literally grew up together. We met in middle school, graduated from high school together, have pictures from every single school dance, told each other we loved each other, went on family vacations, and spent holidays together—we did everything, together, for years and years. He was all I knew and I thought all I would ever want. Cute, right? Or maybe cringey to some of you.

When I say we did everything together, I mean it. During that time, he was my first kiss, we said I love you like we thought we knew what that meant, and he was the first person I was intimate with. Looking back, though, we had no idea what love actually meant. Or maybe my idea of love has just changed (and when I say 'maybe,' of course it's totally changed). I don't think we knew what it truly meant to love another being, to be "in" love with someone's soul and spirit. I think you can love someone and not be "in love" with them. But back then, how could we know this? It made us happy to believe in that possibility. We said that we would get married one day, have a family, and live happily ever after. I held on tightly to how "cute" it would be to marry my high school sweetheart. To have all these hopeful things come true. I thought to myself what a great story that would make. However, in doing so, that made me blind to the many reasons it wouldn't work out that way.

After high school graduation, he didn't want to go to college, and I ended up staying at home for two years and doing the community college thing. I loved doing this because I was able to spend a lot of time working and saving my money. Which, at the time, was very, very important to me. Although we lived in the same city, just fifteen minutes from each other, it was very normal for us to not see each other during the week.

Eventually, I got the itch to do something big. I needed to get out of the house, out of Ohio, move somewhere magical, and do something with my life.

This is when I decided (kind of out of nowhere) that I was going to try out for the dance team at The University of Las Vegas Nevada (UNLV). Sure, I'd seen the college campus on a vacation my family took one year, and I thought it would be cool to go to school there, but I really didn't think too much of the idea until one day, it popped into my mind again. I made the decision that even if I didn't make the team, I would take the plunge and move across the country regardless. I thought to myself, "If I don't get out of Ohio now, I never will." And to be honest, I stand by that statement because here I am now, back in Ohio.

As I made this decision, a couple of things came up for me. I was so nervous that something would happen with friends or family while

I lived 2300 miles away. I couldn't stop thinking about someone dying or someone getting sick. I couldn't stop thinking about my friends not wanting to be friends with me anymore or me not making any new ones when I moved. On top of that fear, I initially didn't want Boyfriend Number One to move with me. That should have been a red flag to me that something was off. However, I ignored it, which is typical for me.

I specifically remember a conversation we had. I told him I wanted to experience college for the first time. All of my friends were off having their college experiences, and I'd never had that. I told him that didn't mean I wanted to explore guys but simply live in a dorm and make new friends—you know, college stuff. I figured it was easy enough to just come visit me and that he could jump on a plane once a month to do so. Eye roll, Alexa. Who has the money and the time at nineteen years old to fly across the country to see their girlfriend every month?

Because we'd been together so long, he wanted to come with me. He didn't like the fact I wanted to experience college and also knew he wouldn't be able to fly across the country once a month either. Eventually, it felt "easier" to have him join me, and there was safety in him being there.

So, he moved to Vegas with me.

THE SHIFT

Once we moved and got settled into our new lives, our schedules were literally opposite of one another. I woke up at 4:00 a.m. to go to work out, took twenty-one credit hours at a time in school, went to dance team practice, and also worked. He worked in the night club, which meant most days he wouldn't come home until 6:00 a.m. when I was already gone for the day. I got really used to being independent while also being in a relationship. I did my thing, he did his, and although we lived together, we rarely saw each other, let alone slept in bed together because of our schedules. This felt normal to me because it was all I knew. I wasn't even aware at this point in my life that this wasn't the type of relationship I wanted.

I seemed to always let things slide because he moved across the country for me and felt like I should because of that. I felt like I couldn't ask for more even though initially, I hadn't even wanted him to move with me. Deep conversations didn't happen, and like I just said and if you know me, you know how important a deep conversation is to me. This man didn't like coming to watch me dance, spend time with my family when they came into town, or meet my new friends. All of a sudden, though, he had made friends of his own from work that I never got to meet. He didn't want me to meet them. Our sex life was non-existent, which to me is very important way to connect with your partner. It pains me to say I was very much the one that lost the interest. Our quality time continued to dwindle. We were going through the motions and hanging on to the story that we were the cute high school sweethearts that moved across the country together and thought that they'd one day get married.

Eventually, there was an even bigger shift. Details I will never quite forget as hard as I try to. It's funny (kind of) every time I open up about this story, everything feels completely obvious. But as I know, when you're in it, it feels so impossible. You feel completely blindsided. More than anything, though, you feel alone because everyone around you can see it so clearly, and most people have no problem telling you that. Those people don't mean to make you feel bad, although they usually do. They come from a good place, but them sharing with you how easy it should be to walk away makes you feel stupid, small, and empty. At least it did for me. I wasn't willing to just give up on eight years. To give up on someone who had been such a vital part of my life regardless of the red flags and the writing on the wall. It's not as easy as it seems or looks from the outside when you are seeing it and feeling from the inside.

It was November, a couple of days before Thanksgiving, and he'd told me the night before that he lost his job at the nightclub. He was going to go back home to Ohio for a while, and he was leaving the next day. I remember saying and thinking, "You can't just go home, we live together, we have bills to pay, we're in a relationship, and Thanksgiving is in like two days. What am I supposed to do with no family here?" I didn't get a choice, didn't get a say, didn't even get a real conversation about it. His flight was already booked, and he promptly left the next day.

Shortly after I got a call from my mom that my sister and sister in-law, Nikki and Mindy, had seen him at the grocery store looking quite cozy with another girl. I wasn't the jealous type and didn't think too much about it. When you're in a relationship this long, you develop a lot of trust. You have to. I never felt a ping of jealousy with him, and maybe that was part of my problem. Maybe there was also a piece of me that just didn't want to deal with the possibility that it could be true.

But, because of my family's concerns, I texted him. "Hey," I wrote. "Nikki and Mindy saw you at the store with another girl and they're a bit concerned. You looked a little too comfortable apparently. Who was it? What's going on?" This made me uneasy, but I couldn't wrap my head around it being real. I couldn't wrap my head around the consequences if it was real.

He promptly sent a picture back to me of a girl that fit the description of what my family saw and told me that it was his friend's (who I didn't know) girlfriend. I believed him because … why not? I had no evidence that I shouldn't believe him and honestly, I can't lie for shit, so I have a really hard time understanding how others can lie so easily.

While he was back in Ohio, we barely talked. Sitting here right now, I really can't even remember us even texting good night or good morning or even catching each other up on our days. I remember one Facetime we had when he thought we should "take a break." I told him we weren't having a conversation like that over Facetime and that I would be home for Christmas soon. So, we waited. I wish I would have listened, but I was someone who didn't believe in taking breaks. Either be with me or don't, but at the time, I didn't want something undefined.

When I got home for Christmas, that was the first time that there was a picture of him and I in the living room at my house next to a picture of Nikki and Mindy and my mom and dad. I told him that when I saw that picture, it was the first time that I didn't picture him at the end of the aisle when I got married. That one hit him deep. It hit me deep, too, but it was the most honest thing that probably ever came out of my mouth up to that point. However, we continued to pretend it could work out, that we would be happy again, that this was "normal" growing pains in a relationship this long, and he eventually came back to Vegas after the New Year.

As soon as he came back, I left to go to Florida for college nationals for dance team. Now, my dance team was good, and it had become my life in Vegas. The year before, we had won a national championship, and this year I was in the center of our hip-hop routine. For those of you who don't know much about dance, being in the middle was a big deal. I did not need to be distracted. I'd worked my ass off for that spot. While at nationals, we only got our phones for ten minutes before bed so we could stay focused. My coach meant business, and so did I. I wanted to win another national championship, and I needed to prove to myself that the thing I was spending so much time on mattered.

My ten minutes were spent calling Boyfriend Number One to say hi and bye and catch him up on the nerves I had for the next day … only on this call, he tried to break up with me. Wrong timing? I'd say so. I was trying to win a national championship the next day; there was no way I was letting him break up with me! And I said just that while hanging up the phone. Sure, there's never a right time to do shit like this, but at least consider the timing.

We didn't win that year, and the disappointment was heavy. We went back to Vegas, and this was when my life was about to turn into a giant shitstorm. I came back to the boyfriend that didn't feel like my boyfriend and had a heavy credit semester at school. One week later, I got the phone call that my dad died. Unexpectedly and completely out of the blue. My boyfriend and I's problems were now the last thing on my list of priorities, although clearly they weren't high up on the list anyway.

THE PHONE CALL FROM HELL

The last time I saw my dad was that week prior on the Florida trip. He took pride in always being there to watch me dance, and I appreciate the hell out of my dad for that. Those are some of my favorite memories. When I said goodbye to him before I got back on the bus to go to the airport, I never in a million years would have thought that that would be my last hug, my last smile, my last "see you soon, I love you!"

I was devastated when I got this call. I mentioned this call in more detail in my first book, but for those of you who are just meeting me now, this is what it felt like:

"Everything felt as if it was moving in slow motion, or worse, not moving at all. However, it didn't feel real. I was completely numb. Dumbfounded. Somewhere inside I already knew I was living in my own personal nightmare. This phone call from hell was just that. I didn't get a phone call filled with hopes and future hugs. I got the phone call: "Lex, Dad died." Initially, I didn't move because the room was frozen in time. I was in the daze of my life. I didn't say it out loud because I didn't believe it because my vocal cords wouldn't allow me to say those dreaded words because if I said it out loud it would make it real. I didn't cry because I couldn't. The tears just wouldn't come. **Until the moment I did move. Until the moment I did say it out loud. Until the moment I did cry.** That was when my entire world came shattering down. When everything I thought I knew disappeared. When I wanted to collapse to the ground, curl into a ball, and hide for dear life. That was the moment I never felt more alone, more unsure, and more scared of anything in my entire life. That was the phone call from hell."

After this phone call, I flew back home for the services. If you want to know those details, check them out in book one, but you'll hear a little bit about it now. As it pertains to Boyfriend Number One, who flew back home with me, he was there physically, but emotionally and mentally he was beyond checked out. I quickly wanted to get back to normalcy, so after a week of being very much in my dad's death, I flew back to Vegas to avoid the pain and get back to my life. I was in difficult classes that semester that I'd now missed over a week of. I was missing dance practices which meant I wouldn't get to dance at basketball games, and overall, I needed to get out of the gloom and doom that is Cleveland, Ohio in January.

When we got back, shit was uncomfortable living under the same roof as my boyfriend. I was sad. He was distant. It was terrible. We slept in different rooms and barely talked. We were hanging tightly onto hope and our story per usual. Eventually, my coach at the time knew we were having issues and also felt for me during this time of grief. She offered to let me live in her casita in the backyard of her family's home. I was able to save money, be around family, and take space from my boyfriend. All of that was needed at the time, and both he and I felt like it was a good idea to take this space to see if it would help us reconnect.

One random night, about a month after I moved out, I got a message from a girl on Facebook. She went to high school with me but was older, and I didn't know who it was. I didn't know her personally but knew my boyfriend was "friends" with her at the time. Again, after eight years, I wasn't really concerned with female friends. I trusted that I was his girlfriend, that I was who he came home to at night, that we had a home together, had moved across the country together, and that our history outweighed any other pretty girl out there.

I should have paid closer attention. Sure, it's easy to look back now and think about how obvious it was that she probably wasn't just a friend, but at the time, avoidance, trust, distractions, grief—they all played a much bigger role than I really noticed. My attention went elsewhere when it should have been locked in to what was happening right in front of me.

She messaged me, "Are you and Boyfriend Number One still together?" I felt weird about it and texted him to find out why she would be asking me this. When he told me she was crazy and to not worry, I obviously began to worry. No man can say a girl is crazy and not actually be the crazy one. (Of course, that's only my opinion, not a fact, but if you know…you know.)

I checked her Instagram and to my surprise, she posted about twenty pictures in a row of them from the past six to eight months. Pictures of them out to dinner, on dates, in bed together, and the gifts he had bought her (ones that matched gifts he bought me, how clever). My heart was shattered. I sent him a screenshot of her profile with a text that read, "Don't worry about her right? She's just crazy."

I called my best friend Maire and my mom in shock. I couldn't believe it. I played the last eight years over and over again in my mind thinking what a waste of time it was now. In the moment, it felt so easy to be done with someone like this. I felt like I was going to be such a badass and so strong, but sadly, that's not the way it turned out. I was broken.

The next day, I went back to our apartment promptly at 7:00 a.m. because I knew he would be back from his new job at a new nightclub by then. Since the last time he and I had talked the night prior, I had received about eighty emails from this girl of videos (yes videos), pictures, and screenshots of the full-blown relationship they were having. My stomach literally churns just thinking about it.

Through the emails she sent me, I found out that that's why he went back to our hometown at Thanksgiving. It wasn't just because he lost his job; it was because he wanted to give them a try as well. She was also the girl that he was with at the grocery store. Duh. Her house was the one he was staying at while he was home, and I later found out that she would come into town—into Vegas—and they would either get a hotel together on the strip or stay at our home when and if I was out of town (like the nationals trip he tried to breakup with me on). Sadly, I never thought anything of it because again, I was used to us not sleeping together, and it's not like he told me he was getting a hotel on the strip with some girl.

This is the shit that people who think it's so obvious don't see. They aren't in it like you are. If this is you now, was you in the past, or is you in the future, please don't beat yourself up for not seeing it. No one else feels your emotions or has the history of the relationship embedded into their heart like you do. You'll eventually figure it out, just like I did. It just takes time and self-compassion.

I also found out that they had a bank account together, and while I was paying our rent from my savings, he was buying her presents, giving her money, and paying off their credit card together. I found out that for Christmas that year, he'd given her the matching diamond necklace to the diamond bracelet I got. What a thoughtful guy. Nothing like a two for one deal, right? Then there was Valentine's Day. He sent us both flowers followed up with cards that said I love you and a million other sweet nothings and empty promises written inside them.

Sure, this shit hurts. Typing it makes my blood boil. I go back and forth on thinking "I was such an idiot" to "of course you couldn't believe it was true." However, the real kicker—as if you thought I gave you many already—is the screenshot of a text message she sent me. The text was from January 27, 2014. The night my dad died. The text read something along the lines of, "What do you want me to do? Her dad just died. I feel bad."

Let me remind you he was my boyfriend of eight years. My dad was a huge part of his life, and while I was grieving my dad being dead, he was in the other room feeling bad for himself, texting his other girlfriend. There was so much distance in this moment. Looking back, it hurts me knowing he couldn't even be a friend to me during this time. His being was elsewhere, nowhere to be found, similarly to my dad's.

This was the first encounter I had with pity. For someone to stay with me because they "felt bad." That hurt, and honestly, it still does. There's more, though. When we went home for the funeral, I'd specifically asked him to stay at my mom's house with me because I needed support. I needed love and if anything, I needed a fucking friend. I so vividly remember him saying, "You just need to be with your mom and sisters right now." So, he didn't sleepover, and I remember telling my best friend, Sara—who came home from college for the funeral—how upset and annoyed I was with him for this. He came to the wake, stood near me at the funeral, and he helped carry my dad's casket with my uncles (yes, he was even a pallbearer—that's how much history we're talking about) and yet he couldn't bear to sleep next to me for a couple of nights.

Here's the kicker, the one that still on a human level hits so deep. I later found out that he slept at his other girlfriend's house every night instead of staying at mine. What in the actual fuck is up with that? In the moment, it was a fight where I had no fight in me. I was too emotionally exhausted, as anyone would be in this situation.

Here I was at the age of twenty-one losing both the men I thought were going to be in my life forever. The man I thought I was going to marry and the man I thought would walk me down the aisle to meet him. Poof. In an instant, everything I knew was gone, and the story that I subconsciously began building was, "All men I love leave. They all walk away. Something must be wrong with me or destined for me." I now sit here, clearly seeing and understanding why I have such a fear of abandonment when it comes to the men in my life. It all started here.

Despite what he did, I tried again. I wanted it to work so badly. For a long time, I thought it was because we'd invested so much time into each other. I didn't know how to do life alone, and it scared me to think I needed to. At that time, my idea of love was that someone would complete me and take care of me. My identity was wrapped, twisted, and intermingled with this man. My excuse was, "C'mon, I think we all have to go back to an ex once to know why we shouldn't do it again." Or, "Don't you believe in second chances?" Barf.

Now, I realize that I wanted it to work out so badly because no one from that point on, no other partner of mine, would ever meet my dad. From that point on, I would always talk to people (especially future boyfriends or dates with new men) about my dad in past tense. My future husband would only know him through stories and pictures, and that broke my fucking heart. It still makes me sad anytime I start dating someone or getting feelings for a person knowing that whenever I decide to have them meet my family that a chair will be missing.

LESSONS FROM BOYFRIEND #1

Time doesn't matter, loyalty does.

Doing big life things together doesn't matter, supporting and being there for each other does.

Saying I love you doesn't matter, being and acting with love does.

boyfriend #2

Earlier in this book, I touched on the idea how a lot of us avoid love to avoid pain, or how we avoid pain by getting back into some version of love. I've done both; I just wasn't willing to admit it until now. However, this chapter specifically is based on me deciding to avoid pain by getting back into love. Not the other way around. Now, I will say I fell in *head over heels love* but at the expense of not feeling most of the pain that was lingering and waiting for me from the death of my dad and the ending of that first relationship.

We live and we learn, or sometimes we just live, and fuck up, and fuck up again. Regardless, it's better than nothing and in my experience, I always do learn eventually. It typically just takes a lot of trial and error. It's so important for us to tune back into our experiences so we can actually learn something from there. This work can get icky (it did for me), but I now see and feel things on such a different level.

My next introduction to potential love happened fairly quickly after all of the other stuff. I was giddy, but it was confusing for many reasons. Still, it made me feel good inside, and that made me want more of it. It made me crave this person and being around him.

Because I was avoiding pain, I enjoyed the new butterflies and smiles this person brought me. The feelings happened suddenly, but the actual relationship itself took some patience. I was nervous to be with someone so soon after my breakup but also couldn't deny how good it felt to be wanted by someone. It felt good to be treated better than I had been for those last months in the first relationship. The shitty part about this relationship was that while it felt so good for me, I was willing to really hurt a friend in the midst of it.

The start of this relationship was way out of character for me. I would say I'm a loyal to the core human, but when faced with the heartbreak I was going through, I was basically willing to do anything to make myself feel better. My heart stings when I bring this up. A lot of us subconsciously do this. We don't know we're applying a band aid. It's okay, we're human. I needed to get out of my head, and I needed hope that I could feel love again, that I could smile again, that I could be loved by someone again.

So, what was out of character about the start of my relationship with Boyfriend Number Two? We were a secret for six months. I don't recommend this. It sucks. It's exhausting, and it eats you up inside. I can't lie for shit, so I genuinely don't know how I did this.

This secret was my decision, not his, which may be karma for later on in life. I was embarrassed, not by him but by the fact that I was hurting a close friend, a teammate of mine who had dated him prior. I totally fucked with "the girl code." You know the girl code, right? How you should never date a girl friend's ex (especially a teammate you were trying to win a national championship with who you saw literally every single day). I royally screwed that up, that's for sure.

About four months into the relationship, she found out. Just like I thought she would be, and also why I was also avoiding this conversation, she was angry, upset, and pissed off at me. Rightfully so. I remember telling her I was sorry when she found out, but I don't think I meant that apology until now. That feels so gross to say out loud. That apology was weak on my end, and I was in a season of selfishness. I was in a season of needing distraction. I was in a season of needing help but pretending I didn't.

Outside of us being a secret, which was not fun, the actual relationship itself was fun as fuck. I always describe this guy as my favorite ex because I laughed my ass off with him, and we rarely fought. He was my best friend at the time, and I truly enjoyed spending my minutes, days, hours, and nights with him. Even so, I unknowingly kept him at arm's length. Which means he had no clue about this either.

He played baseball in college at UNLV which made me believe that my dad would have loved him because of my dad's love for the game. It felt like they had a connection without ever getting the chance to actually meet each other. I rode on this idea the entire relationship. Not to mention, it simply made me feel closer to my boyfriend because I not only actually knew something about his life that was important to him, but I also really enjoyed it.

Because he played baseball, our relationship was long-distance for six months out of the year. He played in college but eventually got drafted to be in the minor leagues. His dreams were coming true, and I was so happy to be along for the ride.

I didn't know at the time, but I now realize why I loved that distance so much. Sure, it sucked a lot of the time, and I missed him like crazy, but it also gave me my independence. I still got to have girl time, I woke up and went to bed when I wanted to, I worked almost every day while he was gone and it didn't matter because I couldn't hang out with him anyway. Sure, I would have preferred for him to be with me, but not always having to consider someone else was nice.

The distance we had to deal with also felt safe to me because if it didn't work out, I wouldn't feel the heartbreak as badly (or so I thought) because he was always gone anyway. That fear of abandonment I gained from Boyfriend Number One and my dad leaving wasn't as apparent in this relationship because it just felt normal for him to be gone all the time. It felt normal for our focus to be on him and his professional baseball career.

The big difference in this relationship versus the first was that we didn't really talk about our potential future together. Some of that had to do with how up in the air his baseball career was, some of it just being young, and some of it that we deep down just were living in the now and okay with it.

Not only was he my best friend, but his brother became one of my best friends, too, and I adored his family to pieces. I often question if I ever really loved Boyfriend Number One because he hurt me so bad, but this one? I know I loved him to my core. I know I was in love with him.

When we broke up, I knew it was coming. I felt the shift leading up to it and could feel myself protecting my heart by slowly disengaging and slowly standing up for myself a bit more than I would have prior. There's always a fucking shift that happens; it's simply whether or not we decide to ignore it or follow it, and if things get better or worse in the short and long term.

I don't have terrible things to say about him. Like I said, he's my favorite ex (if I had to pick one), and yes, he was my best friend. He did turn into a total jerk at the end for a hot minute. My empathy got the best of me. His baseball career ended, and I was in full support mode. His world just got turned upside down with the worst thing that'd ever happened to him, and I wanted to be the "supportive girlfriend" even though a shift toward my own dreams was finally happening.

I haven't really told anyone this before. But here I am, about to tell the entire world, or at least the part of the world that reads this book.

When he called to tell me he got released from his contract, I panicked. I panicked because I knew he wouldn't know how to handle it—of course he didn't know how to deal with this!—but I also felt my independence slipping through my fingers. He'd be coming home five months earlier than I anticipated. Which meant the plans I had for myself—the not considering someone else—was about to change. Talk about a selfish thought. It was also a red flag, pointing me to why

I maybe shouldn't have been in this relationship at this point. You shouldn't feel like your independence is being taken away from you just because someone is your partner. But I gave more to others than I asked for in return, and in my bones, I knew I'd do that again.

He came back to Vegas a couple of weeks after we got the news. We did our best to pretend that life wasn't *totally* sucking for him at the moment, but things were different. There was distance, there was sass, there was an identity loss, and there was a lot of me feeling unappreciated and alone. I felt like I couldn't celebrate any of my wins because he was so down on his losses. That's a tough place to be in during a partnership. You start to resent the other person a bit, at least in my experience. If there's one thing I hope for in the future, it's that I can be with someone that shares my wins even when they're down and vice versa.

The day we broke up, I knew it was coming, and I didn't even fight it. I had no fight left. We were out for a friend's birthday the night before. He wasn't really enjoying himself to say the least, and I wanted to enjoy myself (good for me, go Lex). So, I did just that. I pin-balled my way through the night, chatting with friend after friend. That pinballing was due to the amount of alcohol I had. Not my best, but definitely not my worst. But Boyfriend Number Two wasn't drinking that night, so he wasn't having as much fun "dealing" with my drunk ass. He wasn't very kind about it, either. We fought a little when we got home; he didn't want to sleep with me, and he was annoyed I had the spins.

The next morning he woke up to go work out. I opened my eyes and before he could leave, I said, "We need to talk when you can later. How you treated me last night was not okay." I couldn't have been *that* drunk and remember how poorly he acted. He came back, kissed me, and said, "Yeah, we do," and walked out the door.

I spent the day in my good friend and roommate Kristin's bed, crying and telling her we were going to break up. She didn't believe me. She said, "Everyone goes through shit. You two love each other; it'll be fine. Just have the talk and it'll be over with."

He came over later that night. None of my roommates were home, and I figured he was coming over so he could leave when he wanted. When I opened the door, I laid my eyes on his face and knew the conversation we were about to have was goodbye. I was right; my intuition always is.

He ended things that night because he "needed to figure himself out but loved me so much." Blah blah blah.

I let him talk, then I told him, "I will tell you how I feel, but I'm not chasing you because I've done that before and I'm not doing it again. So if this is it, this is it."

We ended things, and he jumped into his next relationship right away, if not (and most likely) during. That hurt, but it is what it is.

I was left wondering why all the men in my life, the ones I loved deeply, left me. What was wrong with me? It didn't help that they instantly jumped into life with another girl. Was it easy for them to leave me and move on? How could they just move on to another girl that quickly? I felt like I wasn't enough or clearly must have been asking for too much. I felt really alone, used, and betrayed. I felt unlovable.

A MUCH NEEDED RELATIONSHIP WITH MYSELF

Clearly, as I stated, I went the route of avoiding pain by finding love with this second relationship. After that, I couldn't do it again. I couldn't fall in love quickly. I didn't want to. This time, I was going to learn my lesson and avoid love because then I would also, in my head, avoid pain.

What I'm learning, y'all, is that avoiding in any and all capacity is what causes the suffering you go through. We have the tendency to break our own hearts more times than not. But again, you live and fuck up until you don't anymore. I figured if I was alone, I wouldn't have to deal with the pain of heartbreak again. Yay for me! After an eight-year and a three-year relationship, I decided it was time to start running away from love all together. I was going to start dating. My heart went from my sleeve to guarded with a key that I would throw away and forget about. I told myself I needed to have a relationship with myself—which I do think we need but only with the right intentions. Not with the intention to avoid love but with the intention to love ourselves.

Later on I realized it wasn't love I was disinterested in; it was the pain that comes from love that I was disinterested in. However, I can't stress this enough: love doesn't cause pain; the suffering we put ourselves through when we feel like love is missing is what is painful. Love is and can always be present. Love does not cause pain. Please stop confusing this.

While I was alone, young, and single, I sure had my fun. I do think we should all experience this season of life, if possible. This is where my love of travel came into play. I wasn't traveling to see how beautiful the world was, although I quickly realized it is. No, I started traveling so I could once again avoid something: avoid running into my ex, seeing him with his new girlfriend, or out with our mutual friends.

I also started to travel because I figured that's how I would "learn" about myself. I mean, that's what everyone says, right? You hear it in the movies all the time. Wrong (kinda). It's hard to learn while you're actually traveling because you're taking so much in. The new cultures, the new environment, the experiences. Maybe this is just a me thing, but I think you learn about yourself when you stay put after your travels. When you have time to process all that you thought you learned while you were away.

Single Alexa didn't just have fun and travel. Single Alexa also went through one of the toughest couple of years of her life. These tough years looked something like this. Boyfriend Number Two broke up with me a week before my twenty-fifth birthday. Everyone says what a dick move it was, but honestly, I'd rather that than someone who's not really there.

After the breakup and a party girl phase (whoops), I ended up having back surgery at the age of twenty-five. Lucky me. I'll tell you more about this later, but ultimately, this was a dark period for me. A dark period that lasted a long time. I don't think many people knew how dark it was. I did a good job hiding it. I deeply hated myself and my body. I lost my identity, and I didn't want anyone to know that I was feeling this way. I was the positive, optimistic one that helped everyone feel better. Who was going to help me feel better?

I continued to run away. The avoiding never seemed to stop (literally—this is when I moved into a van and traveled the country). I pretended I was afraid of commitment even though I really was just scared of heartbreak, of pain, of suffering. I actually am so down to commit to things.

Instead, I kept reminding myself that being alone was safe. I was going through the motions, focusing on what society told me about love and dating instead of focusing on what I actually wanted, what I was actually doing, and the patterns I was unknowingly developing.

I think you learn most about yourself when you're forced to stop or slow down. For someone who doesn't like to stop (or even slow down for that matter), I truly think it took a worldwide pandemic to force me to feel my grief and to wake the fuck up to all the things I'd experienced.

If you're anything like me, try to give yourself some grace here. It's not your fault that you're human and can only deal with one thing at a time regardless of how well you think you can multitask.

August 10, 2021

Disappointment comes from our expectations of ourselves and the perception of what we think others' expectations of us are

LESSONS FROM BOYFRIEND #2

Falling in love should be fun.

Laugh with your person often.

Real conversations are important and necessary.

Some of us truly do need and want our partner to go deep.

Distance sucks even when you tell yourself it doesn't.

Be best friends.

When you know, you know; trust whatever your heart is telling you.

Don't say sorry when you did nothing wrong.

fear means you're interested

We naturally want to run away from fear. Starting at a young age, we're asked what some of our greatest fears are in life and as children, we respond with things like spiders, heights and ghosts. Things that make us squirm, could physically hurt us, or mentally scare us. As adults, we've learned we can be scared of a lot more than just spiders, heights, and ghosts. Many times, we're scared of things we can't actually see at all. We're scared of things like love, failure, heartbreak, success. More times than not, that fear holds us back from a lot of potentially wonderful opportunities.

Sure, fear is defined as something painful—real or imagined—or something to be afraid of. Of course most of us don't want to go near fear! But what if I told you that we should welcome it? That you should allow it to have a seat at your table. That you should allow yourself to feel fear and embrace what comes along with it. That you should allow fear to move with you instead of staying clear from it. I think if we allow it, fear might actually be guiding us to our highest selves. You may think that's a bit looney of me, but I believe it in my core.

Fear is a constant test, one that's ultimately teaching us. In fact, I'm keen to think it's one of life's greatest teachers. It's a necessity and a non-negotiable. If we avoid fear, we avoid living. We'll find ourselves constantly running away from hard things and big feelings, and when we do, new opportunities of growth and change are lost. They're lost until you decide to look fear in the eyes (yes, as if it's a person) and say, "Hi, it's nice to meet you." I know you don't want to believe me (I didn't want to believe me for a while) but as humans, we are hardwired to do those big, hard, and scary things.

So instead of those childhood fears of spiders, our truest fears are much deeper. They are rooted into our soul, from our life experiences, and they have a tight grasp on our minds. These fears come in the form of change—whether that be a change in the immediate, the short, or the long term. I'd say for most of us, change alone is terrifying. Sure, sometimes we crave something new (like a massive haircut after a breakup), but most of the time we stay living in a state of comfort that comes from minimal change.

Think about it. If you never do life co-existing with fear, you won't do anything at all. Most of us are scared to do almost anything daily, or at least the first time we need to do something. We haven't been here before; of course things are scary.

Maybe I only speak for myself, but I'm scared to do something more often than I'm not. But if I always choose comfort, what am I even doing here?

Rather than us deciding to take the leap, we often allow the fear to paralyze us. We tell ourselves that we'd rather sit in paralysis than potentially take a fall. That fall being your idea of failure. I know it's cliché, but I don't really believe in failure. I think you can, if you are willing, learn something from those undesirable or lesser of the good outcomes. Staying put is not why we're here on this planet. The business of living does not come from staying still 24/7.

Right now, you might be facing unknowns and uncertainties at a fast pace. These changes may make you feel uncomfortable and confused, and I'm with you, friend. However, your fear is there for a reason. It's a feeling that allows you to decide for yourself what is worthy of your attention. Your fear is taking up energetic, emotional, and mental space not to annoy you but because it's showing you that something underneath the fear matters to you. You just need to take the time to pay attention to why it actually matters so much to you.

Fear means you're interested and that your mind is at least a little curious. Which, in my opinion, is one of the most fun, playful, and interesting places to live. When you look past those surface level fears and look into the deep-rooted fears that you carry, it's important to acknowledge why this fear is showing up for you. Acknowledge your fears and take note of them. Maybe you fear one of the following:

- Leaving your corporate job to pursue your own business or side hustle
- Starting a family
- Being in a committed relationship
- Social settings and meeting new people
- Looking at yourself in the mirror
- Time, or the lack thereof

Fear might actually be revealing a hidden desire of yours or showing you something you may need to heal deep inside of.

I know you don't want to agree. I know your mind is telling you something different. Hang with me.

I like to think that we fear the things that we want most, the things we're intrigued by, the things we want to be proud we could overcome. Think about something you feared but tackled anyway. Didn't you feel proud? Did the fight or flight response in your body go away eventually?

Right now, think about your biggest fear. Maybe it's something I listed above and maybe it's not. Whatever it is, really think about it. Now, gently open your mind to the idea that you're about to give fear a seat at your table. Let this fear be seen. Hear it roar. Look it in the eyes, and let it take up a little bit of space in your mind. I'm going to ask you to go into that fear. To make it your friend, not your enemy.

When we think about this fear, our ego—our sense of personality and self-esteem—starts talking. Our ego wants to protect our body, our time, and our environment. When fear pops in, it checks in with that ego of yours, the self you consciously refer to as "I."

As I mentioned, I think fear is an excellent teacher. When we allow fear to teach us something about ourselves, little by little, we stop letting our self-preservation ego have such a strong voice. By doing so, you get to change the narrative from what is keeping you in check and from the outer world. Paying attention to your fear and not dismissing it means you get some of that power back. You get the control to make the decisions and to move as slow or as quickly as you'd like.

Fear isn't going anywhere, especially since it's attached to change, which is rapidly happening in all of our lives. Every day is different, and each day brings us something new to look forward to (I hope you look forward to that). This daily change also means fear also gets an opportunity to show up daily. It's here to remind you that you may need to be challenged or simply just need something to look forward to that is new.

In life, we're constantly faced with the questions that require us to decide what's better or worse for us. Would I rather do this or that? What makes the most sense and what doesn't? Typically, your inability to have a conversation with fear inhibits you from making a decision all together.

There's your ego again. That self-preservation, I, doing not what is always best for you but will protect you in the moment. Remember, fear is a rapid-fire emotion. It doesn't last long. This quick feeling either pushes us to act or signals us to walk away. It can show up in a couple of ways. Facing fears doesn't mean you're not allowed to be scared; it means you're doing something brave regardless of how scary that something is.

As you sit at the table with fear, try saying this: "Fear, I see you. I hear what you're saying. I've played all of the scenarios in my head. I feel you deeply. However, I am going to make this decision. You can get in my pocket and come along with me. We should coexist and get cozy together because neither of us is going anywhere. In fact, I want you to stay as a reminder to me that I am overcoming you." Boom, baby.

I know that sounds silly, but I decided to start looking at fear like it's a person (as well as all of my other emotions). Kind of like in the Pixar movie *Inside Out*. When I look at fear like it's a person, I give it more grace. I come at it with empathy. Your emotions just want to be seen. Just like you. You are dying internally to be noticed, to be seen. Think about the saying, "Treat other people how you want to be treated." Start by treating your emotions how you want to be treated. Otherwise, they'll keep coming back stronger and with vengeance each and every time.

We fear things for a couple of different reasons, and it's important for us to understand what those reasons are. If you don't understand why they're showing up, it makes it really hard to face them. Ask yourself, "Is this my fear or someone else's fear?" Then, name your fear. By naming your fear, you chose to understand it, and you decide whether or not it's your fear personally or a projection of someone else's.

Once you build this awareness, you have a choice to make. How deep am I willing to go right now to figure out what this fear actually means to me? Why the hell am I actually so scared of doing this thing? When you do this, when you do have the capacity to go deep you move toward true alignment, it won't be fun, but it will be empowering.

CHASING MY DREAM

Now, don't get your panties in a bunch. I get that it all sounds nice for me to sit here and say just put the damn fear in your pocket and move on. No, I'm not saying just do it and move on. Of course you're gonna go back and forth, back and forth on making this decision. Again, that's human of you. I'm saying *pay attention*. Don't just dismiss it and never do the thing.

A couple of years ago, I decided to buy a van almost on a whim. I had just started taking traveling more seriously and following my dream to be a speaker. I was just getting back from a trip in Iceland (if you have never been, you should; it's my favorite), and I headed straight to Arizona to speak at a student leadership conference.

This particular weekend, I met another speaker, Mike Smith, who is now a near and dear friend and overall one of the most badass human beings I've ever got a chance to spend time with. It was at this student leadership conference that he and I had a conversation about becoming a speaker. He was down to give me some advice and met me at a local Starbucks. We chatted for hours, trying to figure out what the heck it was that I truly wanted to do (this feels like a daily occurrence).

Finally, Mike looked at me and was like, "Alright, dude, you talk about livin' the dream, you wrote a book on livin' the dream, you tell people how to do it, but are you living yours?" The call out was loud and clear. Now, he didn't say this to me in a rude way. He was honest, and I needed to hear it. Mic fucking drop.

I looked at him and said, "Well shit. I guess not." I told him that I more recently had been looking into vanlife. For those of you that don't know what vanlife is, check #vanlife on social media and you'll get a decent idea what this lifestyle looks like. Of course, take it with a grain of salt because social media has a way of glamorizing shit like this. But vanlife is exactly what it sounds like. It's when a person decides that they want to live in a van and travel the country. Many people "outfit" their vans by making them completely livable with a kitchen and a bed.

Mike said, "Well, what's holding you back from vanlife then? If that's you livin' your dream and the thing you're known for and you don't have a reason not to, then what are you waiting for?" Again, ouch. Fear is the reason. Fear is why I didn't think I could or should do it.

I was scared. Scared I wouldn't be the speaker I wanted to be, scared I wouldn't actually like living in a van, scared that I wouldn't have the money. I was just scared, and my subconscious voice was strong as hell at the moment. Fast forward a month later (yes, only a month later!), I bought the van. I said fuck it to the fear, I put it in my pocket, and I did the thing anyway.

Now, doing the thing doesn't mean the fear just goes away. That'd be nice, but that's not how it works. No, I co-existed with that fear for a long time. Almost daily.

After I made the decision to completely change my life, everyone else's fear came crashing into the picture. When you allow other people's fears to also have a seat at the table, it really clouds your personal judgment on the thing that was desirable about going for it. Here are some of the questions I asked myself:

- Am I scared or are my people scared?
- Am I scared or does society tell me I should be scared?
- Is there evidence or proof somewhere in my life that I should be scared?
- Is the outcome of doing it scared worth it to me?
- What if it did work out?

Once I got clear on my narrative, I continued to do the work on going for it. Anytime I'm super scared to do something, I somehow magically forget about all the times I've survived the other thing in live that were scary. We get so focused on the current fear that we pause for too long.

Something I like to practice when I'm scared is making a list of all of the things I was scared to do but did anyway. Whether I liked the outcome or not, it's physical proof of my bravery and proof that I'm still here. I still have a pulse regardless of doing something scary. Reminder: fear has never killed you. You're still here.

SURVIVING FEAR

Time for some perspective and maybe a little tough love to help you realize how many times you've already faced some pretty serious fears.

Think about this: how many times have you "survived" fear? If you're reading this book right now, you've already survived 100% of your fears. I know this because you're sitting here reading a damn book right now. So you're either not doing anything scary or you're doing it anyway.

Not only have you survived 100% of your fears, but you've survived 100% of your days. I know some of them haven't been easy—maybe some of them have been really hard—but take a moment and pat yourself on the back for being here despite the bull shit life has thrown your way. This means you're capable of doing it again and again and again.

Now, just because you faced the fear doesn't mean you got the outcome you'd hoped for. We can't go into fear (or anything, for that matter) expecting everything to go according to plan. That's not the reality we live in. The only thing I care about for you is that you do your best to face the fear.

For instance, when I decided to have my first big girl purchase—a.k.a. buying a van that I was going to turn into a home—I was scared shitless and questioned myself every time I did a task for it. I was scared but chose bravery. I would never take that experience away. I most likely wouldn't live in a van full-time again, but I'm still here despite the fear.

When people found out I was about to embark on this adventure, many people couldn't believe that I was going to do this alone because of how "dangerous that is for a woman to do." I quickly realized that that was their fear, not mine, and I had to make a decision if I was going to let myself carry that or not.

Next up for me was anytime I decided to enter into a new relationship after having a couple of "failed" ones. Well, I did it anyway. I haven't liked the outcomes, and many times the pain I felt from facing that fear totally sucked. However, I'm still getting closer and still learning. I'll try again (regardless of the risk and pain) because love is worth it, and I still have a pulse. I'm still surviving, always will.

I fear the relationship thing because I have personal proof that up to this point it hasn't worked out. That fear was mine, no one else's. I also heard the noise from friends that relationships are hard and suck at times (their words not mine) so why waste my time dating in this generation? That's their fear projecting on to me. However, sometimes we aren't brave enough or even realize that it's not ours and it attaches to us tightly.

Next, writing not one book but two. Talk about a terrifying experience! I did it, I did it again, and I'll do it again. The fear won't go away even though I've faced it more times. However, outweighing the fear of vulnerability is worth helping people to me personally. And, once again, I still have a pulse. I'm still surviving.

When I published my first book or got onto a stage to speak, many people couldn't comprehend the idea of getting that vulnerable with people (mostly complete strangers). I knew the stories I was going to share would be difficult to put into words, and I knew I'd be nervous; that's why many people don't want to publish books or get on stage. But overall, I was (and still am) willing, able, and excited to do those things even with fear in my pocket.

When fear is present, it might be triggering something inside of you. Maybe it's even triggering something you thought you were "over" but aren't. That fear will keep coming back until you face it. It may not feel like a gift, but it is. The reminder is a gift that will push you toward peace one day.

Do you fear starting that side hustle? Is it because you were told that the only way to have stability is by having a consistent, 9-to-5 job and healthcare? So now you second guess yourself and feel like an impostor for even wanting to try. Ask yourself, "Is this fear mine, society's, or someone's in my close circle?"

Do you fear starting a family of your own because you grew up in a dysfunctional family environment? Because you see how difficult it is for some people to get pregnant and you're scared you'll have to deal with that emotional turmoil as well? Or because you think there is no way that you could be a good parent? Ask yourself, "Is this fear mine, society's, or someone's in my close circle?"

Do you fear being in a committed relationship? Maybe that's because you've been cheated on. Past partners have been non-existent. Your parents didn't have a good relationship, or it was so good you don't think you'll ever find that. You've never received the love you gave. The fear of being hurt again leaves you alone and heartbroken. Ask yourself, "Is this fear mine, society's, or someone's in my close circle?"

Do you fear looking in the mirror? Maybe it's because society's standards say you have to look a certain way. Maybe you don't know how to be kind to yourself because the thoughts in your mind are telling you that you aren't worthy. Ask yourself, "Is this fear mine, society's, or someone's in my close circle?"

Do you fear time? Maybe it's because you have lost someone you love. You know how suddenly a life can end and ultimately carry abandonment with you. Maybe it's because you feel like you are never productive enough. Ask yourself, "Is this fear mine, society's, or someone's in my close circle?"

The list goes on and on and on. Welcome your fears. Fear might actually be trying to tell you something. Maybe that:

- You're ready and wanting freedom.
- You are your own person. You get to decide what type of parent you want to be.
- You deserve love.
- You want to feel like you're enough, to see yourself how others see you and feel the love you give.

- You want to live to the fullest. You have things you want to do, places you want to see and memories you want to make.

When feelings of fear come, so does opportunity. Once you acknowledge fear and welcome it, you give yourself the opportunity to learn more about yourself and to heal from past trauma or unlearn what society thought was important. Once you lean in, you allow yourself the chance to grow.

When fear feels like too much, go back to your interest and the proof of possibility. Please take the word impossible out of your vocabulary. It's not impossible to face your fears, whether those are fears of starting something magical or ending something horrid. Possibilities land in your mind, and your imagination is enough to give that possibility some attention.

If you have a dream that you've been holding on to—let's be honest, you've probably wished for it, seen it in "the wild," day dreamed about it, watched someone else do it, fantasized over it, and imagined it. Deep down, you know this thing you want is possible. Yet there is something in you that says it's not for you. You keep saying it's impossible. Please stop that right now! Guess what, friend? That is a lie you're choosing to tell yourself repeatedly. It's time to see the proof of the possibilities.

I challenge you to make a list of all of the things that you want but think are impossible. Now, make a list of all the people who are doing some of these things. You now have proof right there that it is possible and it is for you.

Sure, even seeing the possibility can be scary. That alone can trigger some fear. But what if something ended better than you imagined? To know and be aware that scary things can end wonderfully? That they can exceed expectations regardless of some coming up too short?

Next time fear shows up, remember your interest. Remember to say hi to your fear and put it in your pocket and keep on keeping on.

September 8, 2019

Fear, it's a feeling to show us we're alive. More importantly it's there to show us we want to be alive. The thing is fear shows us first hand that we have something to lose. That we're not finished. That there's way more to be done. Fear is a feeling we hate and for good freaking reason. It's the feeling of your heart literally beating outside of your chest. It's super high anxiety. It's your hands not being able to stop trembling and where you look down and can physically see them shaking. It's when you feel like you just ran a 6-minute mile and can't catch your breath. Fear is when things flash right in front of your eyes. It's a feeling we wish didn't exist. I think fear, though, is the tell all. Fear is what helps you find your way after you have to face it head on.

November 18, 2019

I think you just need to try and see what life and death means to you and whether or not your fear of living or of death are connected.

January 3, 2020

Dear Time, you scare the shit out of me because I need you and I don't want to need anything. I know I don't have an infinite amount of you, but I wish I did. I know I have to use you wisely and sometimes I don't. Time, be gentle with me but not too gentle. Keep shaking things up to remind me that this is just an irrational fear that I just need to keep taking one day at a time, maybe even one second at a time.

June 15, 2021

Do the scary thing friend, do the scary thing. We all want to be courageous, but we forget that means we have to do courageous things. That we have to be brave. Just like learning to swim meant swimming, just like learning to read meant reading, learning to be courageous means practicing being courageous. One scary thing at a time.

Missing something that never showed
I don't miss you
I miss the version of you I made up in my mind
The you that showed up when you were afraid to lose me
The you that was never ready for me

you don't have to do it all alone

For quite a long time, I thought I could do it all alone, and I mean *it all*. It seemed easier that way, and sometimes it still does. Because it felt easier, I became an independent person.

I embraced the type of independence that leads you to believe that you don't need people to help, support, or love you. The type of independence that makes you constantly question people's motives, morals, and overall character. The type of independence that starts to guard your heart, your feelings, and your life as a whole. I know I'm not alone, but I'm starting to think that we don't actually have to do this alone.

I went from thinking I knew exactly what I wanted in a partner one day to saying I didn't need one at all because for a long time, the thought of being with someone made me cringe. It hurt me deeply because I couldn't see the possibility that someone existed who met my standards, hopes, and desires. I didn't believe that I could count on someone to show up for me let alone to be emotionally available. That idea felt absurd.

It's scary how heartbreak and the way society conditions us can be so damaging, that those can make us avoid opening up about what we really want in our lives. It's taken many years of that heartbreak—many of what some would call my failed relationships—to realize what I want *does* matter even if it doesn't look like what everyone else wants. We do need people, we do need love, and we can't do it alone.

FORGIVING AND LETTING GO

It's taken me a long time to have the guts to share this. To share that I think not only do we need people—because asking for things like help or support feels impossible to me most of the time—but that we also need someone to share things with intimately. For someone to know us like the back of their hand and for them to just overall have our back and vice versa. That's fucking special.

The reason I haven't had the guts to share these thoughts is because I felt stupid wanting a somewhat fairy tale ending. I felt stupid having hope that someone would actually want to stick around not just for a month or two, not just for a year or two, but for my forever.

Constant hurt led to my hardened heart and icky mindset around relationships and love. That hurt changed me in ways I don't like to admit. That hurt forced me to get comfortable with being alone. It stuck around and continued to remind me how broken I was.

There is some risk in being *that* comfortable being alone. I created a not-so-fine line between being okay being alone and forcing myself to stay alone because I was too scared to put myself out there. When you do this, you just pretend that you're not getting lonelier and lonelier.

Y'all, no one gets a trophy at the end of life for being the best single, alone, independent human being that ever existed. That's ridiculous to type out, but I'm a competitive person, so I felt like if I couldn't do anything else right, I could at least do this! I didn't need a man...or anyone else for that matter. I could do it all myself. Even change the oil in my car and a number of other things I would naturally want to ask for help handling. Instead, I got resourceful. I got stubborn. Deep down, this wasn't what I really wanted, but I chose surface level (which is so not me). I'd shaped my heart into something unnatural in ways I don't like to admit.

This entire chapter was drafted in my brain and the notes section of my phone before it even made its way close to being on these pages that you're reading now. Like I said at the beginning of this book, though, I'm trying to take my armor off. I'm trying to show a bit of strength out of vulnerability, out of honesty. I'm dying to know who else is like this. To have gone through much heartbreak and then decided to just avoid catching feelings or counting on someone ever again. I know I'm not alone in this experience because I know there are a shit ton of people experiencing the disappointment and hurt I have.

I hope you (and I) know that it's okay to want a person. To love another human being so well, so fiercely, so deeply. To soften your heart a bit. To re-shape it once again. To crave another human being that you hope to fall into nirvana with. Guess what? You're not weak for wanting to find this. To find your person—the one that supports you, respects the shit out of you, that makes you feel safe and loves you forever—that's what *being* human is. Humans aren't meant to exist solo; they are meant to coexist with other beating hearts, locking eyes, and connecting hands.

It's okay to be tired of doing it alone, and it's even more okay to admit that you're tired of doing it alone. If you're anything like me, I didn't want to admit that I was wrong or that I was ready to find my person. I felt like I got so good at being alone that it made me so nervous to tell people that it was actually time for something more. A deeper connection. Consistent connection. It's been really hard to convince myself that it's okay to want this connection.

If you've been burned by relationships, it's easy to go back to the attitude that you don't need anyone because in the moment, it truly does feel easier that way. And while I might not "need" a man, I do kind of want one. I'm personally a woman who really enjoys a man's presence.

The way they smell, the way my hand fits in theirs, the chemistry, or how I can basically curl up into bed and fit into the spot under their arm. However, a man is not everyone's cup of tea. As you read this chapter, please swap out "man" with whoever you enjoy most. And if you aren't romantically inclined, maybe this is a best friend or platonic partner. Substitute in whatever fits your life and needs.

IT'S TIME, I'M READY

When you go from having some pretty serious, long-term relationships with others, the thought of being alone can become terrifying. You lose your identity, or at least some of it. It becomes easy to love someone, and let's be honest, it feels really fucking good to love someone. To always have someone there to call, to hang out with, to talk to. So then, when you're faced with doing life "alone" and you need to start to doing the opposite, being alone is…terrifying. Eventually, you start to create new habits, make new friends, and have new hobbies. Just like you did when you got into the relationship.

For me, my favorite thing about being alone was that I could leave my phone in the other room. I didn't have to check in with someone, and I didn't have to consider someone else's feelings when making plans or simply wanted some alone time. I could stay out as late as I wanted and go home as early as I wanted to.

When I'm romantically with someone, I am all eyes, all feelings, all everything on this person. I'm loyal as fuck. And while learning to be alone was initially a hard adjustment, it became my favorite thing pretty quickly. After I adjusted, it made it really hard to see myself giving up my independence for someone again. For someone to possibly disappoint me—again—while I invested in them and their life. *This* was the problem. I held onto that narrative that all men were like all the men I'd dated. I now know better, or at least I'm hoping for better. This fear ran deep, and I began to shut things down before they even started. And if they did start, I shut down catching feelings and bounced back and forth between avoiding someone and codependency.

I went from living in a van and swearing off men to a pandemic that brought me back "home" to good ol' Cleveland, Ohio, the place that I didn't think I would ever end back up in. But when push came to shove, a lot of things and circumstances changed. I began to fall in love with being close to my people and my family again. Especially the joy I felt being so close to my nephew, Jameson. When I first came back, I moved in with my mom, my sister Nikki, her wife Mindy (who I like to call my sister wife), and their one-year-old Jameo (my little buddy). Now they have triplets on top of just Jameo. Talk about a hell of a lot of estrogen under one roof at the time, though!

I went from living on my own for eight years, traveling the country, and living in a van for a year to being back under my parents' roof. Let me tell you, that was a fucking challenge and a difficult adjustment. I had to start paying attention to peoples' feelings and space. To consider someone other than me. My alone time was minimal or subjected to a single room, and my business felt like everyone's business.

It was really uncomfortable to not have my own space. Although I was grateful that I had a safe place to land and family and friends that loved me, I was also really excited, in need, and very much ready to get my independence back. During the pandemic, I felt like I had to count on people. That I had to ask for help mentally, emotionally, and financially. I struggled with that. I struggled because I am a sweet yet stubborn soul. I liked the fact that I'd been "adulting" on my own for years. That I didn't need to fill everyone in on my business or ask for the help I truly needed. I felt that if you asked for help, people kept tabs on it, and that made me uneasy. It left me feeling like you always had to give something back of greater value. It made me believe that people would hold it over my head for life. Because of those beliefs, counting on people was and still is uncomfortable and scary for me, as I'm sure it is for many of you too.

Finally, after a year of living at my mom's house, I was ready and also able to do things on my own again. Mentally, emotionally, and financially. It was time to rent my first ever home completely alone. No boyfriend, no parents, no siblings, no roommates. Just me, myself, and I paying the bills and living under a solid roof. I'm really proud of this.

One thing I realized about myself from all of the travel I had done was that I wanted to live somewhere walkable or bikeable, somewhere that had a sunset view close enough to my home, and a city filled with local things like coffee shops and bars. Cue my cute-ass neighborhood that I now live in. A stone's throw away from one of my favorite coffee shops, a bike ride to the lake with a sunset view, and access to so many local shops, restaurants, and bars that are easily walkable or bikeable. I feel like I made it. When I looked at the house I now live in, I was sold instantly by the city and my perfect white brick fireplace, French doors, and white subway tile.

There I was all moved into my very first home alone. I felt like a badass. I felt like I proved that I was making it happen. There I was, being independent again. However, a couple of days after I moved in, I had a moment that forced me to question my independence. I was walking around my new neighborhood in full bliss about the fact that "I did this." I was creating a life that I used to dream of living, only I was living it "alone." I noticed I was using other people's opinions and experiences as fuel, and I subconsciously wanted to show people that I could do it all. There was Alexa's armor again. This tough exterior that wanted to prove to people that I didn't actually need anyone even though deep down I so wanted to let myself want people.

This mentality is always short-lived. The feeling of being okay alone doesn't last very long. You eventually get lonely, and that's a real feeling and beast that you need to acknowledge. Otherwise, the stubbornness will make it come back around time and time again. As I came down from this temporary feeling, I took inventory of my life and realized all of the big, shiny moments—all of my accomplishments and wins—had been done alone. Not physically alone, not even emotionally alone. I had friends and family who have always been there, but at this moment, I was beginning to want to share this with someone more intimately.

EMOTIONAL UNAVAILABILITY

I'm proud of a lot of things I've poured my life into: publishing a book(s), starting a movement, moving into a van and traveling the country, renting this new home roommate free, my first ever speaking engagement, and the list of other cool shit I've had the opportunity to do. However, the common denominator isn't just that I'm proud of these moments. Sure I am. Of course I am. Each one of these things caused some serious blood, sweat, and tears. The common denominator is that I've gone home alone every night.

What I'm trying to say is that I personally haven't shared any of these life-altering moments with a partner, a lover, my person, or whatever you want to call them. The hard thing for me to admit is that I wanted and continue to want to be able to share these moments not just with friends or family but the person who wouldn't complete me but enhance me. Not the one who would try to change me but the person that would make me a better version of myself with the right amount of push. The person that would challenge me and care deeply about what was in my mind and my heart. The one I not only felt lucky to be with but felt lucky to be with me. I am ready for the man that will honor his boundaries and help me honor mine. The one who will love me for all that I was, all that I am, and all that I will continue to become. I am so ready to have this person on speed dial to celebrate with, to cry with, to sit in silence with.

For a long time, I was trying to prove people wrong, trying to make those that left me, miss me or at least wish they were in on what I was doing with my life now. You know, the "glow up" we all have after breakups. Of course I wasn't doing this totally on purpose, but it made me feel a little better than I was in the actual moment. To think, "Hey, their loss." I was putting myself up high on a pedestal because I felt like I could do no wrong.

Like I've said before, I am competitive by nature, but this can get very unhealthy. Many times this nature is simply to fill an icky void and to create a false sense of validation that you're not getting elsewhere. You stop doing things because you truly want to do them; you just do things to make someone else miss you or for them to feel a ping of jealousy or envy.

Here's some examples of my own personally gross subconscious thinking and acting. The first book I published was after Boyfriend Number Two and I broke up. You best believe I thought he would miss being with me when he saw I was finally doing the thing we talked about many, many times. The home I am living in now was after The Situationship I was in ended (you'll learn about this disaster very soon). However, you best believe I thought he would miss me when he realized I was doing something I dreamed of doing when we were together. A.k.a., living on my own. Do you see the pattern? The motivation stopped coming from my own desires and was focused on the desire to make someone else feel like they were missing out. Now, I can see this is as lame on my part. It took the sacredness away from my actions.

Although being alone is okay, and although it's wildly important to be okay with being alone, my point is that you're allowed to want people in your life, whatever that looks like for you. You're allowed to not want to die alone, to have someone by your side who loves you and knows you inside and out. This may seem morbid, but it's true! It's okay to desire to love someone and to be loved in return. It's okay to put the sweet yet stubborn soul to rest for a while.

I think if you got honest with yourself, you'd recognize that deep, deep down, you don't want to be alone forever. I know you can put up the shelf in your house, carry every bag of groceries inside on your own, and aren't scared to live on your own, but do you want to do *all* of that alone? Would it be better with someone else?

Just say it; it's okay. Rip off the band aid. Re-evaluate the idea that success comes from doing things alone. Reconsider total independence as the goal. Just rip those band aids off already! It's human nature to want and need to share moments with people. We are literally wired for that.

Sure, it's important for us to feel proud of ourselves. To feel that if we had to do it alone, we could. It's great to not seek or need constant validation from someone else, but it's also really supportive to know you don't have to do it alone. To be able to vent about something, celebrate something, or cry about something with someone. We're meant to connect, live, and love hard. We're not meant to do life alone, but I know sometimes it feels a lot less painful because we remove some of the risk we may have to experience.

September 13, 2021

I want to be with someone who makes me better. Someone that doesn't complete me and isn't trying to. Someone that enhances my soul, my mind, my heart. I want someone who I feel lucky to be with and in turn they feel lucky to be with me. I think that's how it works, we're both deserving yet loving having the joy of this person in our life.

I'm hopeful for someone who challenges me with the utmost respect, safety and support. Who sees me for me. Who hears me even when there is silence. Who knows me inside and out. Who loves me unconditionally. Someone who truly cares by protecting the shit out of my being.

I'm looking for someone that has sex with my mind and has a deep craving for a below-the-surface connection. I want someone who is on a team with me. Who says yes without thinking but also honors their no's and their boundaries. I want the man that shows up for himself first and me an intensely close second.

I want spontaneous make outs like we are in middle school, skinny dips like we're on vacation and laughs until we nearly pee our pants. I want hugs that are uncomfortably long and tight. I want convos so unfiltered and messy that we need a fucking broom to clean them up. I want breakfasts and dinners and all the meals we can feed our bellies with. I want dance parties in the kitchen and concerts in the car. I want sunrises, sunsets and everything in-between.

I want to feel every single emotion with this human being so that I know that we're both alive. That this is it. That this is the reason for every unfulfilled past relationship. For every broken heart I had to mend back together.

December 16, 2021

What is it that you're so afraid of?

WHAT I LEARNED FROM HEARTBREAK:

Every relationship brings you closer to the one that counts.

You're not wasting time just because it didn't work out.

Breakups are painful, painful, painful.

Most of the time, they always come back.

Don't go backward.

It's not about trusting someone else; it's about trusting yourself.

Your heart will feel love again.

Love is always present even when it doesn't feel like it.

Don't lose hope even when you lose hope.

LOVE REQUIRES ACCEPTANCE ...

Acceptance of possibilities

Acceptance of pain

Acceptance of change

Acceptance of joy

Acceptance of surrendering

Acceptance of anything and everything in-between

Love requires you to say "I accept me for me"

I threw my heart at you and you didn't even try to catch it. In fact, you didn't budge. You stood there looking at me so intently as my glass heart flew through the air. I was waiting. Waiting for your movement. Waiting for you to care, to try, to literally do anything. When it hit the floor you said nothing, did nothing. Which silently spoke volumes. When my heart hit the floor, my voice screamed in agony, dreaming to be noticed. You couldn't handle it though. The heart was too fragile for your hands, too broken for your mind, too open for your soul. You let it drop and you did the easy thing. You pretended you had no part.

the situationship

After having been single for almost four years, I thought I had it all figured out. That's how it works, right? Say you're going to have a relationship with yourself and go do the damn thing. I did a shit ton of traveling, read self-help books, listened to a million podcasts, watched a lot of sunsets, went on some very non-committal dates, went on some hikes, met new friends…that's how you do it, right? That's how you figure out what it is that you want and need in a relationship with another human being, correct? Well, it could be if I'd actually been aware and taking it all in during that time. However, I was just in this space for the "fun" it provided me.

If you haven't figured it out yet, I love to have fun. It's in my nature, and I'm trying my damn hardest to have fun and do hard things. To let them coexist somehow, somewhere. In fact, this year I'm really trying to be more intentional about my "play time" and also the quality of all of my time as a whole.

I spent this time alone mostly committed to the idea that I didn't want anything serious and that I wouldn't put myself out there. I decided that if something happened on its own that felt worth it, I wouldn't deny myself of that opportunity. But more times than not, I shut down the chance anyway. Nothing felt worth it, especially when I knew I was about to live in a van and travel full-time.

In my relationship with Boyfriend Number One, I learned I was decently selfish with my time, my energy, my dreams. I didn't want anyone to get in the way of that, so my ability to compromise wasn't all that great. With Boyfriend Number Two, I did the polar opposite. I gave, gave, gave, somewhat losing my identity in the process. I knew that when it was time for the Boyfriend Number Three, whenever that was, I wanted to meet myself in the middle. To be in the in-between rather than acting from an all-or-nothing perspective.

After living in a van for a full year, I eventually started to get the itch to be with someone. I thought I was ready for love, that I had done the work, got good at being alone, and would be a really kickass partner in crime to someone. Deep down, I really felt that someone would feel lucky to be with me. I'd dabbled with dating apps for pure fun during my single season of life but never had the intention of actually committing to anyone. Having been the person who dated for enjoyment, I knew that now being on the other side of that would be hard on a dating app. It's not something you can always tell right off the bat, and a lot of people aren't honest with their intentions anyway. If you know anything about dating in this generation, it can royally suck. It's exhausting, but again, I'd like to believe that it's worth it.

When I moved out of the van and back to Ohio, I knew I eventually wanted to start dating, that I couldn't just put my life on pause and wait for the "perfect" time. At first, I was genuinely concerned for a while about falling in love with someone in Ohio. It was more of an excuse if anything. I felt like I would be stuck living in Cleveland forever if I found 'the one,' and for a long time, that scared the shit out of me. Gosh, I can be so dramatic sometimes, but c'mon, if you don't know the gloom and doom that is a Cleveland winter, then you can't talk. I eventually got over myself and put myself on the dating apps.

I wasn't sure how dating was going to feel, especially during a pandemic. *Will he hug me?* I'm a hugger. *Where do we go on dates?* Half the businesses in our city are closed, and if they're open, they all close early. *I used to live in a van. Is he going to think that's weird or cool? I live at my mom's house with my nephew and sisters. Is he going to think I'm lazy and doing nothing with my life? I gave away all of my cute clothes when I started traveling. I have nothing to wear.*

These are all of the things that don't really matter, but how can you not be concerned with them before going on a date? It's stressful walking into a place to meet a person you're hoping just looks relatively the same as their picture on the dating app. Then, you're hoping that you look like the pictures of yourself from the dating app and that the other person isn't let down either.

Clearly, I was in my head. To anyone dating right now, I feel for you. Regardless of the many questions going through my head, I thought it was time to find my husband. I knew deep down I deserved to be loved well, but I subconsciously wasn't ready to accept to be loved well. I found myself fantasizing over the first guy I went on a date with. It felt nice to be excited about someone; it obviously feels great to be wanted and even better just being able to get out of the house and do something fun during a pandemic. However, without completely jumping the gun, I figured if this man isn't my husband, he's at least Boyfriend Number Three.

It was finally time to be in another serious relationship, and things were looking promising. I met his family; he met mine. I met his friends; he met mine. We went on trips together. I slept at his place multiple nights a week. He was my boyfriend, right? There was a moment in time I didn't think we had to have a conversation about a title. I figured were in our late 20s and early 30s; adults become exclusive without needing to have a conversation.

Boy, was I wrong. He was not my friend. And in many instances, he actually told the other girls he was dating that I was "just a friend." This was a situationship and a complete fuckery.

If you're new to this idea (like I was), a situationship is a non-committed relationship. However, typically someone (me) will "catch feelings" and want something more. Buckle up; this next thing broke me. In these situationships, there's typically no evolution or growth. Other people are involved, and sometimes you don't know that, or you get lied to about there being other people. There's a lack of consistency, always an excuse, mostly small and dirty talk, one of you says you don't want anything serious, you don't talk about the future, you're frequently anxious, and you get bored. I wish I wouldn't have been blind to what this looked and felt like, but I had been out of the game so long that I didn't know how normal this crap was.

Back to ~~Boyfriend Number Three~~ my situationship. We had our first date. It was fun enough, I was intrigued enough, and I did what all hopeful girls do. I decided instantly not to date anyone else. Mistake number one, Alexa. I don't know about you, but I'm just not the type of person that can date a million (or really any multiples) at once. I get confused, I get torn, I get anxious. If you can, good for you; that's part of dating. But if you can't like me, that's okay too. Both are normal (if you're honest with yourself and the people you're dating).

Of course, being outside of this situation now, I can remember so much being off from the very beginning. In the moment, though, I liked the validation, and it eased my loneliness. On our third date, he told me he wasn't an empathetic person. This may not be a red flag to you, but it was or should have been one to me. I remember coming home and telling my sisters that I wasn't going to see him again. Empathy is one of my number one values, so my partner must also be empathetic. But after chatting with my friends and family, I was easily convinced to give him another try, and then another try, and before you know it, nine months of too many tries.

I remember feeling triggered pretty quickly. Some of the things he said, the way he joked with me, and his confusing mannerisms made me feel all types of ways. Considering I had been cheated on in the past, it was much easier to notice the secrets, the hiding, the typical "you're not the only one" behaviors.

Just because I noticed them doesn't mean I'd learned my lesson. One of my biggest pet peeves with him in particular was the lack of presence he had with me. All we want is to be seen; I don't think it should be that hard. He was always on his phone in front of me, and that always pissed me off. Then followed his lack of emotional capacity and commitment. Of course, I see the best in people. I figured I just needed to be more patient.

So I was just that. I was patient for months and months and months. I waited to have "the talk" about if he was still on dating apps, if he was still seeing other people, and if he wanted to meet my family and friends. I was ready to take those steps but deep down, my gut knew what his answers would be (if he didn't lie), and I didn't want to feel rejection. Because who does? So I pretended not to have the feelings I had and waited a bit longer. I pretended that what we were doing was okay because I didn't want to come off as needy, and somehow I made up the story that I would be alone for another three years if this didn't work out with him.

I also hate confrontation; who doesn't? So we didn't have the conversations right away, but things started happening that made me feel like I was the only one. I started to meet his friends. We took a couple of trips together, just the two of us. At times, he would give me the key to his place. I would stay with him for weekends at a time. I met his family and spent a lot of time with them.

However, this stuff was never reciprocated, which is one of my biggest pet peeves in a relationship. I hate feeling like my stuff, my people, and my life don't matter to my person but that theirs should be the center of both of our worlds. He did the bare minimum—if that. I saw his family almost weekly. He saw mine two times total in nine months. We hung out with his friends often. He only hung out with mine once. When I went to his family's holiday dinner complete with presents and my very own stocking, he refused to come to anything of mine because it was "too far."

The sad thing is I always wondered why I always felt on edge. Writing this out now, I completely know why I was on edge, and I'm feeling a mixture of sadness and anger all at once.

During this situationship, I had no appetite. I lost almost thirty pounds while I dated him. I'm not saying this to glamorize losing weight; I'm telling you because my body was having *visceral* reactions to how I was feeling. I was anxious when I was with him and relieved when I would leave. I would literally get in my car outside his place and take a deep breath. I look back at this girl (this older version of myself) and feel for her so deeply. She just wanted to be noticed. She just wanted to be seen.

Eventually, I did have the talks with him. He assured me he wasn't on the dating apps and that he wasn't seeing anyone else. I always questioned him when he told me what I wanted or hoped to hear, but I believed him because he looked at me dead in the eyes when he told me. Nice move. I figured this was just my body keeping tabs again. That my mind was creating narratives because all I knew was men leaving and men cheating. I chose to believe him over my intuition because I wanted something to end happy. I wanted to be proven wrong that not all men are the same. I craved love so much that I was willing to close my eyes to any red flag that soared through my vision.

He would only tell me he liked me when he was drunk. He only looked me in the eyes when he lied. He made jokes that made me feel like shit. Jokes about other girls and how he was basically God's gift to earth. He always made an excuse anytime I wanted him to do something out of our norm. And any girl I questioned was always "just a friend" and someone I didn't need to worry about. I had reason enough to question everything because my body was trying to tell me something. You typically don't have such a visceral reaction when you just create something in your mind. It's something to pay attention to, or if you're strong enough (I wasn't at the time), just walk away when your energy is being sucked like this.

I know what you're thinking. "Alexa, how obvious!" But I've said it before and will say it again: You don't know when you're in it, and although I do see how obvious it is now, I couldn't for the life of me walk away. I know there are many of you out there who are deeply in this type of situation, and you're doing the best you can. I'm rooting for you to get the love you truly deserve one day.

I danced this dance for nine months, constantly questioning if I was the only one while waiting till I could find actual proof that I was, in fact, not the only one. Again, you have to be strong to not need proof, but it's hard. I couldn't just leave; it wasn't in me. I'd now like to think that even feeling this way is enough to walk, but back then, I just couldn't do it. I wasn't brave enough to trust my intuition over any real evidence. So in the meantime, I started therapy, I lost those thirty pounds because my anxiety wouldn't allow me to eat, I looked like a zombie because I couldn't sleep, I hated facing the day, and I picked myself apart.

There was one weekend in particular that I was really on edge. He was on his phone more than usual, but he did it in a way that he didn't completely hide it from me. Eventually, I saw a girl's name consistently showing up on his phone. I let it slide for a while but just couldn't take it anymore. We had a trip planned for the next week, and I felt so uncomfortable going on yet another trip with him thinking he was still talking to other people that I finally said something.

By this time, we'd met each other's families. This was not something new that I'm being dramatic over. Like I mentioned before, I also didn't feel like we needed to have this "are we boyfriend and girlfriend talk" (although I wanted it) because I was in my late twenties and he was in his early thirties. But, it had been a while, so I didn't know the "rules" of dating. And now, the only rules I want to follow are stay in things that feel good and leave things that don't.

Finally, at the end of the weekend, I said, "Alright, I could bet my entire savings account that you've been texting another girl this entire weekend." He replied, "I have been. Her name is…"

I instantly went into panic mode because once again, he looked me in the eye and proved true exactly what I thought to be happening.

I was thrown off. I thought for sure I would catch him in a lie. It was the girl's name that I'd been seeing on his screen, which made my body instantly tense up. My heart started beating so fast. My eyes started watering. He could see the buildup; there was no way he couldn't, and he knew he had to intervene.

Lie again. He said, "She lives in Florida, and I wanted to surprise you with something nice while we're there. I thought you would enjoy that."

This makes my stomach churn just thinking about it because I instantly can go back to this night on the couch in his apartment.

This was my first panic attack. I remember crying unbelievably hard, thinking that my mind truly was making up all these narratives. I didn't understand how I could get such a gut feeling about this person, and yet he would tell me that I was wrong. This truly was the exact moment that finally brought me into therapy. The moment I thought I was crazy. The moment I thought I needed to learn about trust, and forgiveness, and shame (which I did but not for reasons I thought). I spiraled, but the feelings never seemed to subside no matter how much self-talk and therapy I had.

Because of that, I continued on until I finally got the proof I needed to walk away. Only I still couldn't walk away. He manipulated the hell out of me, and I enjoyed feeling like I finally mattered to him. To watch him chase me for a second. To have the ball in my court. It feels so gross saying that out loud, but I really wanted to feel that love. I wanted to receive *something*. Outside of just getting some validation, it felt so good to see that he actually had some emotions. Who knew? It humanized him, too. He finally told me he loved me (eye roll), and although I didn't buy it, it felt good to have him say it.

I picked up my things from his house, and he continued to manipulate me into changing my mind. Of course it continued. He wasn't used to me saying no, and it drove him absolutely crazy. This is when he pulled out all the stops. All the love bombing and future faking.

We stopped talking right before my dad's death anniversary, and I will never forget the audacity he had to ask me if he could "meet" my dad by taking my traditional Ketel One Shot (my dad's favorite vodka if you're new here) and go to a baseball field to run the bases with him. When I said no, that him doing so was far too intimate for someone that had no respect for me, he showed up at my mom's house with flowers and a card. This is also when he told me he was going to ask me to be his girlfriend when we were supposed to go on an eight-day family vacation for New Year's with his family. The excuses poured through him. He told me to move in, that he was so scared because he thought I was the one, that he had never been in love with anyone until now. Blah blah blah. At this point, I was emotionally drained and tapped out.

Eventually, it came to a halt. We stopped all contact. Until, of course, he texted my best friend, showed up at my mom's house once again, and told me those sweet nothings about how he had changed and told his friends and family the truth about what he had done. I was done playing this game. I finally blocked him and have completely moved on. For the longest time, I was so disappointed about how hurt I was and how I reacted to someone that never even became my boyfriend. I learned the absolute most from this situationship.

What I had to learn when we ended was that *he* was not and is not a trigger. My trigger is my trigger. Not a specific person but how someone treats me and situations I'm in. He simply was the catalyst; I no longer wanted to be triggered by these previous experiences.

For a long time, it was very easy for me and the people who love me to put the blame on him for what I was feeling. He definitely had a part in it; I'm not taking away any responsibility from him. He absolutely should have been better, kinder, and acted from a place of love instead of whatever place he was acting from.

In fact, I'm not taking away the responsibility from any person like that, not in my other relationships or for what you might be dealing with. Treating someone like that is unacceptable. I am, however, trying to share that when we are triggered, it is our personal world showing us what we still have left to heal. These people and experiences are mirrors—if we choose to look at it. It's not about what is 'wrong' with us, fuck that. Nothing is wrong with me or you. It's what we need to heal so that we have space to show up as our authentic selves, to be able to experience the in-between of life without shutting down.

Although we wish others could do this for us because it's messy, ultimately we are the ones responsible for our healing. I'm not saying you need to be grateful for your poor experiences (unless you find that helpful in some way). You're allowed to be angry and hurt by the people who played the villain in that chapter of your life. What I am saying is that you're allowed to also show gratitude to yourself for taking the responsibility of your healing into your own hands. That's not easy to do. It's so fucking hard. And I see you. This responsibility means you can clearly see that you—and me and anyone else for that matter—did not deserve those bad things and that you do deserve the best. You deserve to heal.

This was when I realized it's not about trusting others; it's about trusting yourself. To know that you are smart and capable and worthy of fierce fucking love. That you aren't asking for too much and you are more than enough. I realized that if we aren't aware of our grief, we're also not aware of our love.

PATTERNS, PATTERNS ARE NO FUN

Of course, after looking more deeply into all of these relationships, I finally have opened up to myself. I asked myself, "How do you keep ending up in situations like this? How do you keep ending up with men who disrespect you, and why do you keep staying until they reject you?" These were the questions that kept me up at night.

I now know that we don't intentionally put ourselves in bad situations. We don't intentionally find ourselves reliving patterns just with different people. However, we do go back because the situation is familiar, and with familiarity comes comfort.

Think about it. How do you trust something that is unfamiliar? That's terrifying. So rather than trying something new, we trust what is familiar even if it's painful because we know that if we've survived before, we can survive it again.

That is my truth. A truth I am trying to shift and heal.

While in therapy, I ended up realizing that deep down, I was a person who was emotionally unavailable. Because of this, I found men who were also emotionally unavailable. We linked up like magnets, typically one of us being avoidant and the other being anxiously attached. In doing this, ultimately I knew that these relationships wouldn't last. I just wasn't conscious of the fact that this was happening. Knowing somewhere inside of me that they wouldn't last, there was comfort in knowing that it would end in a breakup and not in death, like my dad.

I protected my heart, or so I thought. Every time I got cheated on or something ended, I put myself on this pedestal. I was the girl who loved so big, who could do no wrong, and who survived every traumatic event in her life with a smile on her face. But I'd had enough of that shit. It was time to come back down to reality, which for the record felt so unsafe.

These types of patterns are hard to break. They are ingrained in us, and we really need help to not only figure out what they are but how to change them. I now find myself in therapy every single week talking about how important it is to feel every emotion. To continuously recognize my patterns and see them when they show up in the now and the future. You deserve to get help with this stuff—or other stuff—if you need it, too. We can't do everything alone.

If you're feeling like you're stuck dealing with the same relationship drama or other patterns in your life try and take a step back, give yourself grace and space, and find someone to talk to. To help guide you to trusting your intuition.

October 29, 2020

I have been scared to cry in front of you, I know what these tears are capable of. I was scared even though I preach it to give you all or none of me. I tried so fucking hard to keep it together, to continue to play it cool. However, I started slipping. I started sharing with you I was anxious, telling you what triggered me, informing you that I was going to start therapy and then before you know it I was on your chest snotting all over that Lululemon shirt of yours and having a panic attack that I was ruining everything.

But, instead of running you held me. You asked how you could help, offered me ice cream and told me I was a good crier. That I just leave it all out there. You told me it was okay that I wear my heart on my sleeve and thank god because the conversation about my dad came next and somehow you laid in bed with me also playing it cool. Keeping me safe from my emotions.

I wanted to die the next morning. To run out the doors because of the embarrassment I felt and instead, you asked to get coffee like we always do. Nothing changed. How?!

Let's be honest; I haven't been that fun to be around. I've created narratives, played movies in my mind and questioned without evidence. I'm aware and trying and I can only hope you stick around for the long haul. That you give this healing Alexa a chance. That we can create more adventures and memories together.

I know your walls are up too, and I'm not sure why just yet, but I continue to hope that brick by brick I will learn why you do what you do and the messy and beautiful things that have happened to make you the man you are today. I can't wait. Multiple people have told me you're a teddy bear and I believe them …

November 4 , 2020

Being around you feels different. I think you look at me differently, it's more intentional. I hope this sticks. That you continue to look deeper into my eyes, that your walls come down brick by brick and you let me love again.

November 9, 2020

What if you're in love with someone who doesn't love you back? Who might not ever? Who may actually not know how? I'm realizing I may not be scared of commitment like I thought. I'm so down to commit, always have been, but I am damn scared of getting hurt again because of committing to someone who isn't ready.

November 18, 2020

I haven't felt this feeling in a long time, so I think I know what it is. I think this feeling deserves a name. Love.

November 24, 2020

I want a partner who wants to show me off. Who is proud of who I am and what I do. Who supports yet challenges me. That makes me feel safe but will do scary things with me. Who considers me and my feelings over anything. I'm not sure if you're capable of that.

December 8, 2020

My mantra has become "always too much, but never enough." I can't stand the inner turmoil I have right now. The constant uncertainty I feel in my confidence or lack of for myself. The lack of certainty in your voice when you say I am the only one. Why can't I believe you?

December 15, 2020

I'm having this intense need for validation and an insane desire to be seen and loved. That's all I fucking want. It's my turn.

December 18, 2020

I'm aware of the pattern now. The pattern of picking men who are emotionally unavailable. The ones who don't know how to see what's in front of them, for the grass to be greener on the other side. It hurts to feel like I am on a hamster wheel of unfit people.

December 19th, 2020

What the actual fuck. I thought I was crazy. I thought I was creating narratives and I wasn't. I should have trusted my gut and instead I named, wrote down, and said out loud all of the things that would make me believe that there was no possible way that it could be happening to me AGAIN. Instead, I believed you when you lied to me. But sadly, there's relief. Relief that I was fucking right. Relief that I'm not crazy. Relief that the familiarity of pain is back and that I know I'll be okay eventually. I want to hate you. I want to scream. I'm angry. I'm so fucking sad, it's almost comical.

December 26, 2020

Fuck you.

February 4, 2021 (the text I never sent)

It shouldn't be this hard, it shouldn't feel like this. I don't get it, at all but I can't force you to tell me the truth as to why you're so scared to commit or to go to that level with me. What I do know is that I am tired of crying over you and having a pit in my stomach. I'm tired of wanting you to want me. I'm tired of waiting around and wondering "is this time finally it" while having no respect for myself in the process. It's all too confusing. You've played with my heart and my mind and I need to take control again.

You're not in this, it's very apparent, it's always been. I was just naively hopeful. I need someone who chooses me and only me. Who doesn't manipulate me and loves me unconditionally - the good and the lesser of it.

I'm sorry I gave you an ultimatum when I should have just walked. I'm sorry I led you on for the last week when I should have stood my ground on being done. I'm sorry I'm not what you're looking for. You deserve being head over heels for someone and I deserve someone to be head over heels for me. I love you and I love your people, probably always will. I want nothing but the best for you. But this is it, this is goodbye.

March 8, 2021

Someone can give you acts of love and not be in love with you. Just because someone doesn't love you doesn't mean you're unlovable.

April 14, 2021 (my birthday)

Decided today I wasn't going to go into another year with shitty boundaries and putting others (especially your) feelings before mine. I said goodbye AGAIN.

April 16, 2021

I keep asking myself these questions. How do you trust something that is unfamiliar? How do you trust something that's never been? How do you trust the unknown?

Honest answer, I don't know but you just do. Maybe you let go and let be. Maybe you close your eyes and do it anyway. Maybe you just cross your fingers and wish for the best. I think we deserve that chance. To just trust the fact that it could be better. Trust the fact that there has to be better. Trust the fact that you don't need to keep surviving your life away. You don't need to remain on autopilot with this flight or fight response. Stop hurting your own feelings. It's hard to watch. We all do it, but today, it's time to stop. It's time to trust.

April 25, 2021

Love never looks the way we think it will and it never feels the same either. The cool thing is, it's not supposed to look or feel any certain way, it just is the way. Lately, I've been having a lot of conversations with people who believe and have said "you are love, Alexa" that it's within us at all times and if you're capable of giving you've been receiving all along.

Not gonna lie, I would tend to roll my eyes. I didn't understand this and it felt plain funky. I thought to myself "love isn't me; it couldn't possibly be me." It's things like *The Notebook*. The couple goals I keep seeing as I am mindlessly scrolling through Instagram. Blake Lively and Ryan Reynolds's marriage. It's the shit Ed Sheeran sings about. It's not me, Alexa Glazer. It looks perfect and feels even more perfect. It's hard to find, easy to lose and there is no chance that love is just me. But guess what? I'm learning it is. I dig some digging and guess fucking what ladies and gentlemen it is me. It's you too. It's in and around us at all freaking times. This love doesn't look and feel like I thought it would but it is perfect. It doesn't have to be hard to find, just look inside.

LESSONS FROM A SITUATIONSHIP:

Don't fucking do it.

Dating sucks.

Trust your gut from the start.

Most of the time if someone doesn't want to show you off it's because they are hiding you from other people.

People lie, even when they look you in the eye.

Getting taken advantage of sucks.

Listen when someone says, "You deserve better."

Just because someone has good people in their life doesn't mean they personally act like a good person.

People are a mirror. They will show the insecurities that you need to work on.

Maybe people deserve a second chance but nothing more.

You deserve big, good, show you off to the world good.

It's all you knew
Don't beat yourself up for falling into old patterns
You went back because it was familiar
You went back because you knew you would make it out
alive no matter how hard it was
You went back because you believed in hope
You believe in people
You believe in love
Don't beat yourself up friend, you're doing the best you can.

your intuition is trying to tell you something

Here's a lesson on trusting your intuition from someone who has a really hard time trusting people's intentions. I think that was pretty obvious from the last chapter. Trusting my intuition has become a practice that I don't take lightly. A practice I honestly wish I didn't have to practice but need to. I want to be able to trust a random stranger, but I'm learning that sometimes you just can't, and you need to trust yourself first.

Over the years, I've bounced back and forth between feeling like I trust people too easily and that I don't give people a chance to be trusted at all. I typically give people the benefit of the doubt right off the bat. Are you like this, too? This has gotten me into "trouble" many times, like in many of my intimate or romantic relationships. I've trusted people time and time again. Those who apparently didn't deserve it. Every time this became obvious, it's made me question if I should start having my guard up. It's made me question if I shouldn't share myself completely with others, or if I just shouldn't trust people at all.

Those options sound miserable. To not trust anyone feels cold. I like giving people the benefit of the doubt. That's something I do enjoy regardless of it sometimes making me mad in the end. I think we all have good days and off days, so I simply don't want to catch someone on an off day and decide then that I will never trust their being or their character again. It just doesn't sound like me, and it doesn't seem totally fair.

This is who I am to my core. Hi, my name's Alexa, and if you didn't realize, I'm a total empath. If you're anything like me (and I bet you're reading this book because you are), you've done this time and time again. It's hard to not get cold after multiple people have let you down. You can't help but start to get a little worried about trusting people in the future.

More recently, I've realized it's not really about trusting other people. What it's really about is being able to trust yourself enough to make the decisions that are right for you. To trust yourself enough to listen to your body, mind, and heart. To know that the right decision isn't always the easy decision. That the right place isn't always the place you want to be. That doing the right thing for you might mean you leave some people behind. It's not about what's right or wrong to society; that's a myth. It's about doing what is right or wrong for you and trusting it with your being.

This is way easier said than done, of course. Trusting yourself typically involves you also second guessing your every move until trusting yourself just becomes the easy answer.

We have to be kinder to ourselves in this process because it's a really hard process to go through. I've tested and tried it. This is hard if you're someone who trusts easily and have gotten hurt or if you're someone who doesn't trust at all. We've all got our reasons. Both make it hard to trust ourselves.

My guess is that, just like me, you have evidence in your life for either trusting or not trusting people. I get it. You've had many people betray that trust, and it's made it really difficult to continue to open up time and time again. Or maybe there have been a couple of times you didn't give people a chance at all because you were so guarded, and you later regretted that. Let's try and meet somewhere in the middle, in the in-between. That middle ground is you getting really fucking confident in trusting yourself.

I know some people think that trusting your gut is a little "woo woo" or just not a thing. But our bodies are smart. They speak to us, and we need to start listening to them. That feeling inside of you is happening for a reason. The changes in your body are happening for a reason. You don't need to have evidence or logic to make decisions if they feel right to you. You don't need to ask permission, and you especially don't need to get someone's approval to make a decision. The more you learn to trust yourself, the more confident you get in being able to make decisions and the less confusion there will be in your life.

BEING AWARE OF THE SIGNS

People come and go from our lives all the time. Kind of depressing, I know, but if you think about it, how many times in your life have you believed someone else over yourself? A parent, a teacher, a post on Instagram, a friend, an article, a partner, or a complete stranger over the internet? My guess without you even answering is that you've believed all of these people over yourself more times than not. What type of shit is that?

You are the one person you will spend every single day with for your entire life. You don't come and go like the majority of the people in our life do. You are not temporary. You wake up and go to bed every day and night with yourself. When you're upset, or happy, or anything *in-between*, you are the only one you can count on to be there with you. It's always been your job to hold space for yourself because someone else isn't always going to be there, and many times their intentions won't be where you want them anyway. You're the only one who has experienced every day, every moment in your life for what it actually is. No one else can possibly know how your experiences have felt, affected you, or possibly even changed you.

That being said, don't you think you should have your own back a bit more? That you should start trusting yourself a bit more? I sure do! Instead of believing what everyone else says to do or not to do, you should start believing in that feeling your body provides you with daily: your intuition. To trust that no one knows you better than you. No one likes being ignored; your intuition doesn't, either.

In my first book, I talk about "signs." Signs from the universe, signs we hope to receive from people that have crossed over. For me, I always really want to receive signs from my dad. I know not everyone believes in this, but it's something I wholeheartedly do. In fact, it keeps me going. I feel like when you believe in the possibility of signs, you move with more hope and a starry-eyed wonder for your life.

I personally think the universe and my dad are constantly leaving me little bread crumbs. The universe and your people are probably trying to do the same for you. Those bread crumbs—the signs— help reaffirm my path depending on how I decide to interpret them. I say "depending on how I interpret them" because I tend to interpret them in a certain way. I perceive these signs in a hopeful way. It's not right or wrong, but it's interesting to take note of this. Sometimes that looks like me trusting a sign from my dad over myself.

I don't blame myself for that. The little girl in me could always use a little validation. She wanted (and still likes) to know that she was making the right decision. I'm still working on this. Working on being able to make even the simplest decisions alone which continues to feel hard for me.

I started to realize that when I was looking at these signs, I was trusting someone else over me. For instance, my dad flickers lights. I always interpret flickering lights as my dad saying, "Keep doing the thing you're doing, it's okay." Rather than, "Hey, Lex, trust what feels right. Maybe that means walking away." Sometimes life requires you to do the hard thing, the letting go, the walking away, the being alone. I never wanted signs from my dad or the universe telling me I should do something else hard.

More recently, I was at a bachelorette party for my best friend from college in Portland. We had a fun group of gals together, that's for sure. There were plenty of laughs, drunken adventures, and spontaneous things along the way (like tattoos). The first night in the city, we decided to stay in, order Mexican food, drink some margaritas, and catch up on everything that had been going on for everyone recently.

I've grown close with my best friend's sister, Kat, over the years. She's a medium. If you're unsure what a medium is, they're someone who can communicate with spirits. I know I'll lose some people here because some just don't believe in this work, but please, keep an open mind. You might feel something a little bit like magic, and it can become such a special experience.

Knowing she was going to be there, I was hoping that my dad would make some sort of appearance. I wasn't going to *ask* her for a reading; I was simply planning to wait and see if he would come through to her. I wanted to make sure my focus stayed on my best friend and her weekend, but deep down I really wanted some guidance. Guess what? My dad showed up for me. His spirit came through loud and clear.

All of us girls were standing around the island in the kitchen when Kat paused. "I'm sorry," she said, "but does a red bird mean anything to anyone here?"

I was instantly giddy. Excitement ran through my veins. This was my dad making a grand entrance! The week following my dad's passing and the funeral, there was a cardinal that sat in the tree of my mom's house. It never moved, not even for a second. It truly felt like my dad was watching over us. Since that moment, any time I see a cardinal, it feels like a pocket of joy and a message from my dad.

After I said that the bird was my dad, Kat asked me if she could do an entire reading on me. She mentioned that the spirit (a.k.a. my dad) wouldn't leave her alone and she wanted to see what he had to say. "I've been trying to tell him to quiet down," she said, "and he simply doesn't want to. Can we do a full reading?"

"Yes, please!" I said, and she went to get her tarot cards from her bag.

During that reading, my dad made it clear that he was around me every single day. Listening, watching, and always trying to tell me something. I knew this to be true; he showed me plenty of signs, and I always ran with them with full appreciation. But what he told her next surprised me. He said that I wasn't listening to what he was *actually* trying to tell me. I didn't understand what that meant.

A wonderful example of this was when I finally had a conversation with the man from that situationship. This was the conversation about whether or not he was seeing anyone else. You already know what my gut said, which was why I avoided that conversation like the plague. This was about three months into us talking, and I'd reached the point that I wanted it to be serious or not and to move on (if only I could have moved on). I sent him a very random text because, again, I didn't want the dread of confronting this in person. "Hey, I'm not seeing anyone else, are you still?" I said. Maybe that text was forward, but when you're ready to know, you're ready to know. My best friend Sara (my best friend from high school) was my hype for this conversation. Naturally, of course, he responded that he wasn't seeing anyone else.

As soon as that text came through, a cardinal flew past us in the parking lot. Sara and I looked at each other, and knowing that was my dad, literally said out loud, "Big Phil, we need more than that! What does it mean?" After the two of us were talking to a bird in the sky, I got another text from this man saying that he was enjoying what we had going on. I looked at Sara and couldn't decide if he was being truthful or not because honestly, my gut still didn't trust him. The bird flew by again, though, and I took this as yet another sign to believe him.

Then, I called my sister Nikki because I had to tell her about the cardinal flying around during this conversation. When I called her to tell her about it, the bird flew by again! My belief came from me not wanting another failed "talking stage" or relationship. I had already invested three months into this guy, and I wanted it to work. Because I wanted it to work that bad, I took the flying cardinal as a sign to trust the guy rather than my gut, which said he was lying.

And that was my problem. I really ran with whatever I *hoped* my dad was saying with these signs, not what he was actually trying to say. He was telling me to trust myself. At least, that's what he was trying to tell Kat as she was giving me this reading.

I'm guessing I'm not alone in this. I bet other people do the same thing. It's natural. You want to have this conversation or get advice from this person, in person, and you can't. So then, you start to imagine what you wish they would say to you, not necessarily what they would say. The thing I learned during this reading was that my dad had been trying to tell me to trust my intuition, that feeling happening so clearly in my body. That's why he told Kat, "I'm always around, but she isn't listening."

Signs from the universe are a gentle nudge to remind you that you already know what you need to do. To trust your intuition. To trust the person you're with forever, a.k.a. you.

YOUR OPINION OF YOU MATTERS THE MOST

This lesson and reading spoke volumes to me because too many times I was focusing on what everyone else told me to do or wanted me to do. I had a really hard time separating advice from my intuition. Long story short (which is not something I do well, I'm a writer for Pete's sake), the guy was lying to me. He lied for nine months, in fact, and I ignored the feeling in the pit of my stomach the entire time. I gave him the benefit of the doubt, I gave him chance after chance, I gave him my trust, and he played with my emotions like a game.

We're always going to be faced with new experiences. That's the point of living, right? Having those new experiences often means we're also going to be faced with fear, confusion, and possibly overwhelm. With that overwhelm, we typically reach out to our friends, our families, our people to get those feelings off our chest. To discuss every pro and every con. We always hope that people are going to tell us what we want to hear, but more times than not, that's not the case.

When we do have these conversations, we open the doors to test our confidence and generally to receive a lot of advice. Some advice is asked for, and some isn't. If you don't know how to trust yourself—which most of us don't—getting all of this advice from others will continue to confuse and overwhelm your decision-making skills and trusting your gut. Ultimately, it will cloud your judgment, and you'll make decisions based on what you hope people would say, what you think would make others happy, or what would have the least repercussions.

When you deal with these types of conversations, I want you to know that it's okay to ask for advice, to ask for a sign from the universe or a loved one, but it's also okay to just hear it, to let it go in one ear and out the other. Most importantly, it's okay to not let anyone else's opinion affect your own. To not let it change your mind or weaken your intuition. It's perfectly okay for someone's opinion to hold value in your heart and in your mind but for you to still choose to do what feels most right for you. I applaud you in trying to figure this out.

Remember: you are the one getting feelings to do or not do things in your life. It's important to get these questions and thoughts off your chest, but please, choose who you do so with wisely. It's natural for us to project what we have gone through or what we are going through in our lives onto others. Because no matter the similarities of someone else's life to yours, your actual experiences will always be different. While we live in a world full of opinions, please know that the opinion you have of yourself, of your decisions, and of your life, is what matters the most.

November 20, 2021

Life hack: Maybe don't take advice from someone who isn't doing the thing that you want to be doing or living the life you want to be living. Stop taking advice from those you wouldn't want to trade places with.

Baggage

We all have baggage.

We each carry around these imaginary suitcases stuffed
with the human experience.

At times, we hope a bag gets lost in transit.

That we never have to look inside again.

We each think that our baggage is heavier than someone else's.

Yet, at the same time we think that our baggage is insignificant
to the world.

We can't have it both ways.

You may pay more for your baggage,

It may be heavy.

But you need it all of it.

going into the basement

I've watched one too many scary movies and have been to too many haunted houses. It's almost annoying how much I love to be spooked in those settings and yet cringe when they feel so real in my daily life. However, when it's not my real life, I love the adrenaline in wondering what's behind the door, in the basement, inside the closet. I enjoy the feeling of my heart racing and my lungs tightening followed up with a laugh, knowing it's not real and just a movie or a haunted house.

Although I know it's not real, whenever I go back to the comfort of my own home, that fake, scary shit never feels so fake anymore. The sounds come out of nowhere, the darkness feels unbearable, my thoughts go wild. It's no longer funny to feel scared when it's happening in real time. To know a noise isn't a "normal" noise you've heard. To think about every detail of every scene from a scary movie or a murder mystery book and wonder if it's about to happen to you. Although the movies, the haunted houses, the mystery books are "fake scary," it always feels that it could be possible in reality. That the spooky character could be hiding in my own home, living in my home, in my closet, or especially in the basement. I don't know what it is about the basement that feels so "off limits," but what I do know is that I always feel like I need a lot of courage to go down there.

I know I'm not alone. Even as an adult, I still don't want to go into the basement, especially at night. I'm not even sure what I'm so scared of, but whatever it is feels justified. I know the monsters under the bed aren't real. I know the boogeyman doesn't exist. I know more than likely it's safe down there regardless of potential cobwebs, spiders, and old storage bins filled with nonsense. However, the darkness, the stillness, the quiet, and the cringey feeling I get in my belly as I'm about to take the first steps always remind me that with the darkness comes the unknown, and with my imagination, anything is possible. So I run. I run down the stairs as quickly as possible and run back up even quicker.

It's funny; growing up, I always envisioned that when I turned the light on, someone would be standing there looking at me, unmoving. Then, whenever I would shut the light off to go back upstairs, the same imaginary person would chase me all the way up. I spent as little time as I could down in the basement as a kid.

As a full-blown adult living on her own, I don't want to spend time down there. Sometimes I completely avoid my basement all together. For instance, in my current home my washer and dryer are in the basement. Doing laundry is hands down my least favorite adult chore on the planet as it is, so the fact that I rarely do it doesn't surprise me. The fact that I also have to go to the basement to do so makes me do it even less. I know I can't be alone. Maybe I'm just one of the few thirty-year-olds willing to admit it.

Think about it. Are you a little on edge when you think about going down into the basement? If so, you're probably like me. If you have the courage to go down into the unknown of your basement, you turn the light on the moment you can reach for the switch, and then you take a deep breath when you realize that the imaginary person, or bugs, or other creepy crawly things aren't down there.

But maybe sometimes you wait. You don't have the courage at that moment. You wait to go down into the basement until the morning when the sun is up because for some reason, we think the monsters and skeletons, the creepy crawlies, don't come out at that time of day. You wait because you don't have the capacity to see what's down there at just any given moment. You avoid it, just like me, until you're feeling at least a little more ready.

I later realized working on yourself is kind of like fearing going into the basement. Sometimes it's really scary to go there, oftentimes you are unsure of what you're going to find, and more times than not you avoid the work all together. When I voiced this to a friend, she mentioned that you don't have to go down there alone; you just have to remember to ask someone to go with you. That's where therapy comes in for me, and maybe for some of you already or in the future.

A trusted, trained mental health professional can help you go down into "the basement." This basement is just a storage zone for all of those patterns, trust issues, relationship problems, childhood trauma, and whatever else you've personally got down there. I know not everyone has access to this support, but it's important that you learn how to unearth this if you don't have access to that help, whether that be a friend or a family member that you trust.

Most basements are used for storage, right? Think of the basement as a place where every single moment in your life is stored. Where every single emotion you've ever felt is living. Where every single person you've ever interacted with has a home.   Well shit, no wonder we're scared of the basement! If you told me all the people from my past are living in my basement, that's reason enough to not go down there. I'd say most of us have avoided some moments, some emotions, and some people for a long, long time. So long it almost feels foreign. Taking steps toward those basement stairs means facing our grief, locking eyes with heartbreak, and overall acknowledging our human experience. I've got the chills just thinking about it.

We avoid the details of our story just like it's the damn basement, at night, after watching a scary movie. We may simply look but not touch and say to ourselves, "We'll save that for tomorrow." We may take the leap and go down there, but as soon as we see or feel an emotion we don't like, we sprint back up the stairs, shut the light off, and slam the door.

We do this on repeat. We rarely allow ourselves to go into the dark at night, to slowly turn the lights on, and observe what we see or what we hear. Most of us are not okay with this type of discomfort. It feels like too much. It's too intense.

I personally know the things that would surface if I decided to go into this imaginary basement and sit in the discomfort of my moments, emotions, and the people of my human experience. I mentioned that I recorded the audiobook version of my first book years after publishing the paperback edition. This was one of the first times I scratched the surface of what real work is on myself. When I read those sentences, chapters, and pages of that book out loud I realized how scared I was to actually dig in. To go into the basement of my heart.

I sat there reading each and every word with tears in my eyes, a pit in my stomach, and a crushed ego. I was emotionally, mentally, and physically exhausted because each memory that came up took me right back. It took my breath away. What I found interesting in this process was how these experiences happened to linger or show up even stronger this time around. It didn't quite make sense, but honestly, it doesn't need to. It just was what it was.

When we learn about grief, about tragic times, about change, many people say that time will heal it all. That each day it gets easier. I think this gives hope at first, but naturally it will cause some confusion for people when it doesn't actually heal or get easier. In my opinion, that's one of the biggest misconceptions of being a human on this planet. Grief, tragedy, change—this stuff doesn't magically get easier. It gets more manageable, but it will always catch you off guard when you least expect it.

As I read my audiobook, I figured that that experience would be one that empowered me to do something greater than myself. That it was going to inspire me to write my next book (this one you're holding in your hands right now) and create something wildly inspirational. Granted, I hope this book in your hands is wildly inspirational but more so, what I really hope is that this book in your hands is honest. That it pushes you to slowly walk into the basement of your heart. That you trust yourself in knowing that there is nothing you can't handle down there.

While I read my words out loud, a lot came up for me that I didn't know how to digest. I was filled with little trust, a lot of resentment, minimal hope, immense sadness, a bit of hate, and a million other things that felt so unfamiliar to me. The thing I realized most about me was that I wanted to be fun and have fun and not deal with anything else that would bring down the fun meter. The process of going down into my heart basement was anything but fun, and being around myself also didn't feel fun. It was forcing me to go into a basement without a flashlight, knowing the light wasn't going to work, and that I was going to have to rummage around blind to find what I needed. *cringe*

As I sat in my parents' bedroom closet, recording this audiobook and feeling these extremely unfamiliar feelings, all I could think was, "I am an optimistic person. I am the livin' the dream girl for Pete's sake! Why am I having such a hard time right now?!" During those months of recording, I felt like the biggest fake on earth. I'm hard on myself (if you couldn't tell), but I now realize I wasn't being fake; I just held onto hope and happiness a little too much when I really needed to be at peace with what was happening.

You know when you don't want to let go of something and your knuckles turn white because you're gripping so tightly? That was me. I white knuckled happiness so tightly. I wouldn't dare let go because I knew if I did, a flood of not-so-happy things would show up. That I would be stuck in the dark with the emotions, experiences, and people I didn't want to face. Eventually, I couldn't stand it anymore. I had to let go. I had to face it. Many things in life can feel like a sprint *or a* marathon. But I knew that this type of work was going to feel like I was sprinting a marathon, and oh, what a challenge the thought of that is.

I was confused, though. I was perceiving myself in one way and feeling another way. I perceived myself as someone who was making the most of their life and their circumstances. I felt brave. I mean, I had just been traveling around the country living in a van by myself! Something most people don't do. That felt like the definition of brave. On top of that, I was doing what felt like a million other things that others thought were brave. I was perceiving myself in a way that I thought (key word thought) I was doing it all right. That I was alive and well.

The world decided to shake things up. To force me to look at the perception I had of myself and to get really honest with how brave I actually was. I went from living my dream, traveling in a van, working remotely, and speaking on stages to students all over the country, to suddenly being forced to drive the van back home to Cleveland, Ohio from San Diego, California because Covid and the pandemic weren't just fake news like I had hoped.

My spirit felt like it had died, and my soul was nowhere to be found. I had very little money, I wasn't happy with my body, I didn't have my personal space, and the lack of mountains and sunsets was a difficult adjustment. Here I was, living under the roof that my dad died under, back in the city where I met Boyfriend Number One, which also brought up a ton of gross and icky feelings, and I was no longer doing the one thing I loved so much: speaking. I couldn't meet strangers or hug my people (and for a person whose love language is physical touch, I struggled). I started looking for validation in other people (a.k.a. The Situationship), and I couldn't stand the person I saw in the mirror or the one constantly talking in my head (the old version of me). I couldn't get out of the funk. I felt zero purpose and was depressed as fuck.

As I lost my grip on happiness, I realized I had no choice but to go into the dark basement. The one where the light didn't work, the stairs creaked, the draft was cold, and I had no flashlight to look for anything.

It was time to sit in the discomfort of the basement of my heart, of my mind. Getting ready to go down there meant it was time to prepare myself to dig through all the storage bins. To pick up every emotion, every past and present person, every life experience, and make some hard but serious decisions about my hoarding.

Doing this is not easy. Letting go and holding on to things so near and dear to you is a nightmare. It looks like picking up storage bins labeled by year of "Alexa's Life" and knowing that inside, I will find many lost memories. Each storage bin will have all the details of every moment in my life, and I now have to analyze what went well, what went poorly, and how to do it better next time (if I even have it in me to do better). The basement is scary, but going down there is a necessity to having a home with structure.

Take small steps toward this on your own. Ask a therapist for assistance with this task. Read books like this that can help guide what you're examining. Listen to podcasts that will help nurture your growth. Surround yourself with family and friends that support you, not judge you. Overall, just know that you can go into the basement, and even if you don't like what you find at first, this work is worth it.

November 8, 2020

A global pandemic, who would have thunk it. The opportunity I now have to feel everything, remember everything and do absolutely nothing but overthink and sleep. I now have all the time in the world to realize every single trigger of mine. Every trauma I thought I didn't have. Look at all this time you have, Alexa, to dissect everything that has happened to you up to this point, to analyze every conversation, every experience, every moment. I remember thinking it was fake news. Ha, joke's on you (and sadly the rest of the world). However, the reality of the situation is that this feels like a mixture of hell on earth and a zombie apocalypse

August 21, 2021

I'm tired of being so damn hard on myself.

Unlovable

You needed to feel in control and I needed to feel rejected
so instead of leaving I waited around for you to put me back
to this familiar place of feeling unlovable.

healing isn't easy but it's worth it

In the past, when I heard about peoples' healing process, I thought that overall, it must be this beautiful experience. This was based on what I saw on social media; very few people shared *during* the healing process and just shared the glory of the end. When that's the only part we see, of course we begin our own healing journeys and suddenly feel like we're literally on fire. It feels extremely heavy, and nothing about it feels light. I used to strongly believe that healing must have meant a newfound ease in life. Which is not the case. Peace? Yes. But ease? Not always. Anyone else feel this way? I don't think I'm the only one who has misidentified what this process could look and feel like.

During my situationship, I started going to therapy. In that chapter, I mentioned I experienced my first panic attack—or the first I could recall—while I was with him. This was the first time I was really aware of how my body reacted to things.

I remember waking up every single day feeling guilty that I felt so terrible inside. I just wanted the anxiety in my chest and in my gut to go away. Rather than going to the source of the issue, I definitely tried finding relief in other ways. I found myself numbing through wine, drinking a lot alone and even in the shower (which felt like a low point that I tended to laugh off). I found myself wanting to smoke more than often, I found myself eating less and less, and I found myself doing so much but nothing at the same time.

Looking back, this makes sense. Collectively as a society, we look at physical pain differently than mental and emotional pain. We're scared that if we agree to healing, we'll have to put our life on pause to heal something we wish wasn't broken or rearranged in the first place. The interesting thing is that we eventually heal our physical pain because we're told we shouldn't experience life "halfway." That if we can't do some physical movement, we'll be living an extremely unfulfilling life. Eventually, most of us decide we should take a break from the thing causing our body physical pain. We rest, begin to take medication for the pain, get the steroid shot, attend physical therapy, and find ways to take care of ourselves if the pain is chronic. We'll even go under the knife if necessary. Eventually, we get the more long-term fix, and we listen to our bodies, to our doctors, and we take time off to recover, to repair, to rest.

I've done all these things for my physical body but when it comes to my emotional and mental health I never seemed to care as much. I had the "chin up, buttercup" mentality. You too? Why? Why is it that our physical vessel is that much more important than our heart or our mind?

When we think of recovering from physical pain, we think there's a deadline to our recovery. When you get surgery, your doctors say that you have to recover for "X" amount of weeks or months, followed by "X" amount of time with a physical therapist, and then you can go about your life as normal. Normal is not the case. For whatever reason, our mind thinks that's it. But healing is not a one-time fix with "X" amount of weeks of recovery. Healing is forever, recovering is also forever. You must be gentle with yourself every step of the way. Healing your mind, heart, and body is a lifelong fucking process. You constantly have to consider if the things you're doing will help or hurt you and you need to adjust your lifestyle and act accordingly.

I am someone with serious back issues (we'll get into that deeply very soon). I know that if I decide to do for a run, I will destroy my back for at least a couple of days. Before I make the decision to run or not, I have to ask myself, "Is this worth the pain?" For a long time I said yes, and I beat myself up for putting myself through that. For trying to prove that I could do it like I used to. The fixer mentality. However, now I say fuck no. Going for a run is not worth it.

For whatever reason (there are a lot of them), we don't look through the same lens when we're feeling grief, depression, or heartbreak. We don't decide to take the break, try out therapy, get on the medication, and do the same things we would do if it was our bodies in pain. We think bringing up therapy or medication for our mental health is too taboo or not accessible anyway.

We also try to adapt the timelines we receive for recovering from physical pain and translate that into how we recover from our mental and emotional pain. However, healing in every realm is hard as fuck. I'm not sure why we think it's supposed to be easy other than we're just trying to hold on to some hope that it doesn't actually feel like you're drowning in the ocean with ankle weights on. In reality, healing takes a really strong, brave, and bold person to be aware of everything that's going through their body not just physically but also mentally and emotionally. To truly look at all these deep, scary, and dark pieces of their being and of their story.

So, friend, healing can be a really painful task. I'm sorry to tell you this so bluntly. Therapy can be a really uncomfortable place but such a sacred experience you get to have with yourself. Recovery can feel never-ending, but I promise you'll feel relief in there.

I understand why few people want to go there. However, just like the back pain, or whatever physical pain you personally deal with, it doesn't just go away without change. It gradually gets worse and worse. Eventually, you can't take it anymore. I deeply understand how these things catch up to us in time. Just as our back pain continues to worsen, so does our heart pain. We forget that many times it has to get worse before it can get better. That healing means unlearning and relearning. It requires adjustments and grace. It requires mental toughness and a shit ton of love. It requires a lot from us; it takes a lot out of us.

HEALING BODIES, HEALING MINDS

Let's solely think about healing when it comes to your body for a minute. The healing process is slow. It's out of our control. It requires trust, patience, and mindfulness. You have the hope that things are getting better, that you took action to feel better. But then, it's here. The action has been taken, and it's fucking hard. This physical pain is also very pressing on your mental and emotional state, especially if you decide to go the surgery route. At least in my experience.

I've had back problems my entire life. From age fourteen, on. It started with some aches and pains, became a stress fracture, turned into a fracture, and so on and so forth. I continued putting off the pain for years while playing with as many temporary fixes as possible. Finally, at twenty-five, I had back surgery. I remember going into that surgery "excited" because I thought I was going to eventually start to feel better. It felt like the right thing to do at that point.

Once I had the surgery, there I was at twenty-five years old, relearning how to walk. On top of the physical things I had to relearn, I also had to learn how to ask for help and ultimately count on people for support. Asking for help is something that I am not good at. I don't think many of us are.

My spinal surgery took place on December 7, 2017. At twenty-five years old, I had the body of a much, much older woman. My back was all sorts of screwed up, which is pretty funny now considering they literally screwed me back together. My L4 was moved 30 percent forward, my disk was herniated, my vertebrae was fractured on both sides, and my nerves had nowhere to go. My body didn't have a place to live comfortably which meant I couldn't live comfortably. After twelve years of back pain that got gradually worse every year, my legs and feet finally went numb. This was my reality check; we all need one.

When you're twenty-five and tell people you're getting back surgery, the unsolicited advice starts coming. The advice to not get the surgery because I'm too young. The advice to use steroids and stem cells. The horror stories of it not working, me waking up paralyzed, or me not waking up at all. Sure, any of these things could have happened, but the truth was that I was too young *not* to have the surgery. Too young to have to live my life the way I was living.

So I made my own decision. The decision to live life pain free one day. To be able to go on a walk and not need to take a break. To sit in the car for a road trip and not want to cry from the pain. I made that decision as quickly as possible. I went under anesthesia for three and a half hours, let my surgeon cut me open on both sides of my spine, allowed him to take my disk out, replace it with a new one, and put me back together with four titanium screws and two metal rods.

Healing is a tug of war between the future and the past. Healing is taking one step forward and three steps backward. It's one of the harshest forms of confusion. It feels like a fucking detox seeping out of every pore of your being. It's painful and unexpected. Many times during this process, it's hard to tell if you're even making progress. That's just the start.

Most of the time, we dread healing because it means we're about to start from scratch. That there will be a slight pause, a bump in the road, and a lot of discomfort.

Get broken up with, start from scratch.

Lose a job, start from scratch.

Get surgery, start from scratch.

Use your entire savings account, start from scratch.

Graduate from college, start from scratch.

Move across the country, start from scratch.

Lose a parent, start from scratch.

Insert anything you've gone through, start from scratch.

I have experience with all of these start from scratch moments, and I know some of you do, too. All of these unnerving, scary, and extremely uncomfortable situations are ones you don't exactly thrive in or get excited about in the beginning stages. Try to focus on starting from scratch as a place of new beginnings. It's a fresh start, a chance to become someone new, a chance to gain strength.

Healing is messy. My hope for you is that you start to see that if you can recover from physical pain, you can also recover from the mental and emotional pain you're going through. The process is similar; you just have to trust the support that you have (or need to find) to help you get through it. Trust yourself that you can get through it.

Back surgery prepared me for the grief and healing I should have already been dealing with but wasn't. It's having to pee in a pan because you can't get out of bed. It's not being able to bend, lift, or twist for six weeks. That means not being able to tie your shoes. It makes it very challenging to put on your own underwear and pants. It makes it impossible to shave your own legs.

It's dropping things way more often than ever in your life because it's such a challenge to pick them up. It's walking with a walker at twenty-five while people give you dirty looks because they think you're faking it. It's not being able to get in and out of bed by yourself. Not being able to drive a car. Oh, and if you don't know this, after the anesthesia, medications at the hospital, and painkillers they send you home with, you can't even take a shit to save your life for about five days.

None of that was fun, but there were also positives of starting from scratch. You have the ability to find a new sense of creativity in your life. It's a way to recreate yourself as a human and take the opportunity to say, "Hey, allow me to reintroduce myself." Even if that means calling yourself Iron Woman because you now have a bionic back (that's what I do).

Hindsight 20/20, I wish I would have looked at my mental health healing like I did my back surgery. That it was something I just had to do in order to make my life more enjoyable. Less painful in the long run. Most likely, I would have done it much sooner.

To the person healing right now: You're in it. Deeply in the process. You're thinking to yourself, "What in the actual fuck is happening right now and when the fuck is it going to be over?" You're probably questioning everything and then some. You're feeling exhausted, alone, and waking up instantly wanting to go back to bed. This experience isn't wholesome. It's not beautiful, nor fun. It's no walk in the park, and you're doing it anyway. That's brave. I wish someone would have warned me that healing isn't the euphoric land of unicorns and candy covered streets.

So, friend, it may not be glamorous. It may feel like we never truly heal. But what I do know is that we somehow stop letting these events, triggers, and moment in time take control. We're able to tell them to kindly shut the fuck up, to simmer down, to gain power back in our life, and eventually, we wake up and get out of bed.

I know you were hoping for rainbows and butterflies. I was too. Please remember that you're doing the best you can right now, and you deserve to heal. I see it, keep going.

April 16, 2021

I keep asking myself these questions. How do you trust something that is unfamiliar? How do you trust something that's never been? How do you trust the unknown?

Honest answer, I don't know but you just do. Maybe you let go and let be. Maybe you close your eyes and do it anyway. Maybe you just cross your fingers and wish for the best. I think we deserve that chance. To just trust the fact that it could be better. Trust the fact that there has to be better. Trust the fact that you don't need to keep surviving your life away. You don't need to remain on autopilot with this flight or fight response. Stop hurting your own feelings. It's hard to watch. We all do it, but today, it's time to stop. It's time to trust.

August 10, 2021

Building relationships with others starts with building a relationship with yourself first. How's that going Lex? I had a breakthrough in therapy today and I'm really feeling the in-between of who I was, who I am supposed to be, who I am starting to feel like or show up as. It's scary, but it's beautiful. I looked in the mirror at all of my perceived imperfections and I've decided to keep what resonates and I'm leaving behind what no longer serves me.

November 22, 2021

Old me wasn't safe and now the new me is aware of that. That's a weird place to be. Because I've never been the new me either. Which means this side also doesn't feel safe. Where do you go when you feel like no part of you is safe?

THINGS I LEARNED AND PRACTICED IN THERAPY:

Crying in front of someone is not something to be ashamed of.

Feeling sad means that I am alive and living well.

Everything we experience in life is temporary, even painful feelings.

It's okay to want to feel love.

You're allowed to change your mind and you don't need to justify it to anyone.

Not everyone is on the same path but everyone is doing their best.

Healing is ugly at first but beautiful eventually.

Naming my feelings allows me to better understand what is happening in my body.

All feelings are valid and important. Big or small.

Boundaries are not optional; they are a necessity.

Self-awareness can be a real bitch at times but it's better than being asleep.

Love wins. Always.

Strength is not putting a smile on our face and telling people you're okay. Strength is crying your eyes out and sharing with people that you're not okay.

close your eyes

Let's talk about music for a second. When you listen, do you listen to the music or the lyrics first? Do you always find yourself stuck thinking about how the lyrics were made just for you? Or does your body start to move to the beat of the song? I always thought I listened to both, but I was wrong.

LISTENING TO THE MUSIC, NOTICING THE LYRICS

It was the morning of my back surgery, and my mom and I were on the way to the hospital. I told her that I wanted to listen to a "pump up song" to get me ready for the journey that I was about to go on. At the time, I was really loving the song "Stargazing" by Kygo. I started blasting the song. When I looked over, I saw my mom was crying.

"Really, Alexa?" she asked as she looked at me. "This is your pump up song? Are you even listening to the lyrics?"

No. I wasn't listening to the lyrics; I was just listening to the music. Sure, I was singing the words, but I wasn't processing them at all.

I heard the music and connected with how it made my body feel. This song put me into a little trance, relaxing me, and making me feel at ease. My mom heard the lyrics about loss, hope, and love. Apparently, not my best choice for the situation and probably not a real pick-me-up when you're about to go under anesthesia. But again, I liked the way the music made me feel. On top of that, I'd already told her I hoped to see my dad in surgery, who had already been gone for several years at that point. I hoped I might get to see him again in that *in-between* place I think you go when you're under anesthesia. Not a good choice on my part.

However, you live and you learn (or at least try to). It was this moment when I realized we each process music differently and a lot of it is dependent on our mood, what we're searching for, and what's currently happening in our lives. The general pattern I've noticed is that if you're happy, you focus more on the music itself because it allows freedom in your body. But, if you're on the sadder side of things, you may pay more attention to the lyrics in hopes that you're seen or heard in those words. This still gives your body a visceral experience but a different one. If you want to figure out your pattern, pay attention to your mood and the music you decide to listen to.

ALEXA, THE DANCER

I grew up dancing, and that very quickly turned into my identity. It started out by me dancing in the aisle ways of the grocery stores and bouncing around in the living room. At age three, my parents put me in my first dance class. We still have the costume I wore on a stuffed Elmo somewhere at their home. After that first class, the rest was history. Every year, I became more obsessed with the art of dance while also wanting to be the very best at it. I eventually went to college to pursue dance and always thought that I would move to Los Angeles and dance professionally. My identity from three until twenty-five was Alexa, the dancer. I loved everything about it. How it made me feel, what it taught me, and what a staple it was in my life. It truly was the first thing I fell in love with and the hobby I basically had a relationship with. Dance came first; everything else came after.

Eventually, that came to a halt due to that back surgery I told you about in the last chapter. I'd had enough, and when I was no longer able to dance and move my body in the way I used to, I really struggled with connection. It was really difficult to connect with my body but also to music for years after my surgery. Dance tied music and I together. It was the glue. Dance made me attach to the way music would move and groove through my body, through my veins. It truly felt like a battery for me. When music was playing I was charged, I could move, I could feel, and I could disappear into this world that no one else knew about—my mind and my heart. I would dance to get through hard days, sad days, inspiring days, all the freaking days. After I had surgery, I felt like I lost this relationship or at least didn't know how to interact with it anymore. If music was no longer in my life to move, then what was it for?

I realized that my entire life, I told stories through my body. My teachers would pick a song, choreograph a routine, and each of us would interpret that story on a stage or in class. There was safety in this. There was safety in knowing that no one actually knew what story I was sharing because we all interpret that movement, that music, differently. I like to say that dance was my first form of therapy because it allowed me to feel in ways many don't. It allowed me to share myself intimately but still in a way that felt safe. It felt safe because it looked like a show, but I wasn't acting at all.

After I had surgery, I realized that I couldn't share stories with that type of safety anymore. This was a harsh reality because it came at a time when I really needed that outlet. I didn't know how to feel in any other way, and after my dad died, two "failed" long-term relationships, and the relationship with dance ending, I was one lost fucking puppy. I knew connection was important to me, but I didn't know how to connect anymore. I'd been practicing and perfecting movement my entire life. It felt so shitty to need to start over. I felt lost. I had to become more open in using my words and using my voice. Not only was this scary, but it also felt much harder at first to get inspired. I realized that I still needed music to help inspire me and begin my storytelling.

PLAYING THE GAME

That's when I started incorporating music in my life in a new way. I would lay on the floor, close my eyes, and really listen to where it would take me without moving my body. This was hard at first. Most of us don't just sit or lay without moving unless we're sleeping. We're conditioned to move, move, move both our minds and bodies all day long. Five minutes to lay on the floor listening to music doesn't seem long initially, but after about thirty seconds, you start to get the itch that you should be doing something more productive.

I started playing this "game" by myself and eventually recruited some friends to play as well. It's for those who enjoy the way music makes you feel but also for those who enjoy being in their mind.

My friends and I would find what I like to call "close your eyes" music (what I started to explain above). In fact, I have an entire playlist on my Spotify dedicated to this "game." This music typically has no words and gifts you with presence, awareness, curiosity, and a state of being. Whenever we found a new song, we'd send the recommendation to the group along with the text, "Close your eyes and tell me where you go." From there, anything was possible.

If you want to play, do the same. Find some of that "close your eyes" music and put it in a playlist. When you press play, make the decision to release all control. In the next couple of minutes, let your mind do the talking and your heart do the feeling. Places filled with adventure, with wonder, with hope. When I play, my mind takes me to places so vivid I feel like I'm there. I can feel the adrenaline. I have chills just thinking about it.

After playing this game for years, knowing the places my mind took me and hearing all the places my friends would go, I've realized how wonderful it is that your mind can do things like this if you just give it the opportunity. To quiet the outside noise and societal chatter. This type of game or exercise lets your mind shut out the world and relax for a few minutes, and in today's world, we need that more than ever.

AWARENESS CREATES CHANGE

Because of the awareness I gained from my game, I started noticing a common thread in the places my mind would take me. This was happening when I lived in the van in my late twenties. I no longer had an array of destinations I found my mind taking me. I used to visit places with wildflowers. I'd be running through the trees, climbing up mountains, speaking on stages surrounded by a crowd. Instead, I always felt a certain way, saw a similar thing, and it always left me feeling like I wanted and needed more.

My visualizations always had me in the desert, always standing naked and vulnerable, with the wind spinning around me, the world moving faster than I could handle, and sadly, I always found myself alone. There were quite literally no other life forms around me. For the longest time, I didn't think anything of it. I'd always enjoyed the quietness of the desert. In fact, I used to run off to the desert when I lived in Las Vegas for some much-needed alone time. I thrived over the sunsets that I experienced there, the way the sky turned into cotton candy, the dirt and sand on my feet which always made me feel grounded to the earth, and the vast openness of the land. I grew to love this pocket of the world because of those seven years I spent living there.

When I started to truly take note as to why I was visualizing this, I realized that sure, the desert was a gorgeous place, but it also became really apparent that it's the deadliest place on earth. Everything is dead, dry, open, and empty. Looking back, I believe that I was seeing this because I was unknowingly living a life that was similar to the desert. One that was empty and dry, I just wasn't aware of it. I found myself constantly surrounding myself with thoughts about death and time—or lack of it. I realized those thoughts were finding their way not just into my visualizations but my everyday thoughts. Once I became aware of this pattern, it made me curious.

These thoughts invaded my head space both consciously and subconsciously. These thoughts about life and death and everything in-between made me question how long I would actually exist, in human form, on this planet, during this life. Not because I didn't want to be here—I really want to be here—but because I couldn't get death out of my mind. The reality of that is because I know how short life can be. I know how it can get taken from you without a moment's notice. That idea was taking over my mind. My thoughts were becoming more morbid by the day.

As I was driving and turning a corner, I would think, "What would happen if my car just fell off this cliff? Would anyone care? Would someone find me? Gosh, my mom would be really pissed if this is how I go ..."

Other times, I would think, "I think I am either going to have a short life and die young or a really long one with no one left in it."

"If I die right now, I'm going to be really pissed because I don't even like what I am doing right now." That was common, too, but so were the thoughts that justified somewhat reckless behavior. "If I die right now, I would at least be doing something I enjoy."

You see, outside of my dad dying completely out of the fucking blue, everything in my life seemed to happen suddenly. Endings always happen quickly, and yet the emotions I had from these moments always were a slow burn for me. I didn't have the capacity to feel them, so the feelings lingered and lingered. While I could never predict endings, I could almost always avoid feeling them after they happened.

This is when I became attached to the thought that everyone leaves, everything ends. Which is true, sure, but to think about that often is heavy. Everything we experience in life is temporary, and forever is always shorter than we expect. Even the happiest of memories, the biggest love you can feel, it all ends in heartbreak.

These thoughts are kind of depressing, right? They might make you feel a little squeamish or empty just thinking about them. They sure make me feel that way. However, I was so concerned about the possibility of it all ending that I couldn't actually be present. Instead of thinking about what could be, I focused on what had been. I focused on my evidence that things end, and they end suddenly, so don't get too attached because you're going to feel like shit if you do. It was a way to cope, to try to make myself feel even just a little bit better.

When I realized I wasn't being present to life, I beat myself up for spending too much time focusing on the "wrong" thing. It's so easy for us to get wrapped into what everyone else tells us to do. They tell us to simply live in the moment, and trust me, I want to, but that's hard. It's hard to trust that what's happening is moving us in the direction of where we want to go eventually because honestly, we just can't know for sure. Instead, we hear, "Stop thinking about the past, stop focusing on the future, just be." You can call me out. I've said it to myself, and I've told other people the same because I wanted to believe that I could make that happen. That "close your eyes" game of mine helps me be present. A lot, actually. It helps even if it's only for five minutes.

Even though I strive to be more present and more at peace with the moment, it can still be hard. It's hard because sometimes your soul takes over. Sometimes you can't stop thinking about the things you miss more than life itself. Sometimes you can't stop thinking about the things you deeply desire most. Sometimes you can't stop dreading the present moment because the present moment feels to be sucking the life right out of you.

This, though, is where we need to wrap our minds around peace. To be mentally free of the disturbances that our reality can potentially bring us. How it shakes us to our core sometimes. We have to train our minds and our hearts to have peace in our presence no matter what comes in. Know that your presence is being wherever your mind is during that pocket of time. That may mean that your present thoughts have taken you to your past or even your future. That's okay. It's fair for us to allow it all in. Honor your thoughts when they show up in the present. Don't force them in; don't force them out.

THERAPY SESSIONS

Eventually, the game I played with music became a staple in my weekly therapy sessions. Only this time we play without music and it didn't feel like a game anymore. In fact, it's not a game at all. It's me going into my heart "basement" for a minimum of an hour every week with someone holding my hand.

It feels intense but always worth the intensity. It's almost like me listening to music in this way was preparing me to be able to sit awkwardly in a room with another human being, with no music, having no crutch to lean on but to be able to close my eyes anyway and go somewhere. I had to try to put words to my feelings and share that experience with someone else.

During my early therapy sessions, it became apparent really quickly that my life revolved around two things: death and love. Knowing the reality that all things end has affected me deeply. It's affected the way in which I feel safe or not. In how I share and feel love. In how I show up in the world. Ultimately, every time I closed my eyes, the grief that I felt from death and my desire to love and be loved was weighing heavily on me. I went from seeing wildflowers and climbing mountains, to the desert, to now a pitch-black room with just me standing or sitting inside of it. Talk about literally having to create a new language for myself.

I always found myself sitting in my therapist's chair, with tears in my eyes, the same sweatshirt I had been wearing for days on end, and a sunken face that gave away the fact that I was exhausted and not sleeping. I found myself sitting there and never once feeling judged by him and the thoughts I always felt too morbid or sad to share with anyone else. This is why therapy or a safe place to land is key for your mental health. You need a non-judgmental break.

Many times sitting in that chair during my sessions, I felt heartbroken and alone until I began to learn how to trust myself. I felt like a fucking idiot for a long time. I felt like I was annoying to everyone else. I felt crushed. Not only was I afraid of the judgment from others, but I also deeply felt this judgment from myself. I was being so cruel to the poor girl that had already had her heartbroken that I was breaking it even more. I wondered why I stayed in relationships. I struggled with the fact that I didn't feel worthy of feeling better or being with someone who treated me like a decent human being. I questioned myself, my love, my intuition, my guts, and my bravery.

Thank goodness we forget what heartbreak feels like when we aren't in it. Although, I think most of us are scared of love because it puts us at risk to get our hearts broken again one day. I think because we lose sight of the pain, we eventually risk it all again, and that's a beautiful thing. That's how you know you're still alive. You risk for the sake of magic in your life.

Closing my eyes all started out with not being able to dance and move my feelings through my mind and my body. It transitioned into a fun game with friends, and now I'm here, still closing my eyes to let my feelings have a place to roam. I'd say this has been the gateway for me to get re-connected to my mind, my storytelling, my body, and everything *in-between*. Thank goodness it's given me the space in a very hectic world to listen, to see, to feel.

I think you should try it. Take a couple minutes to close your eyes to a song that will take you somewhere special. If you need a recommendation, lay on the floor, put some headphones on or in your ears, close your eyes and listen to Essential Attitudes by Peals. Let the magic of your mind and the thoughts you have yet to be conscious of wake up, and share that possibility.

Most of us don't take the time in our days to sit still and be with our thoughts and feelings. Most of us want to go, go, go. I get it, because same. To continue rushing through life because it feels potentially easier that way. If this is you, when you close your eyes, make sure to sit with the discomfort of being still for just a couple of minutes. Gift yourself a window in which you don't have to do anything at all. Your heart will thank you later. Be kind to what shows up and pay attention to what's happening even if it gets a little uncomfortable. Don't judge yourself for the things that do show up. Instead, befriend them and learn from them.

Now, go hit play and close your eyes.

May 11th, 2020

I know the answer, I just don't want to accept it.

October 16, 2021

I'm not scared for people to leave because I expect them to. I may even be standing there holding the door for them.

CULTIVATING AWARENESS LOOKS LIKE:

Catching yourself in the act.

Allowing yourself to witness your own transformation.

Waking yourself up to the idea that changing your life, may mean saving your life.

Allowing yourself to let go of patterns and past versions of yourself.

Being aware that simply feeling, thinking, and acting in a certain way does not mean you're aware of how you're thinking, feeling, and acting.

Recovering people pleaser

Letting go has never been easy for me.

Letting go has always felt like a slow death.

But today, I did it. I let something die.

A feeling of hope that would never settle

A feeling of love that would never be filled.

A feeling of disappointment that would never quite disappear.

Today, I said yes to boundaries and no to you.

I let go of you, the idea of you I so perfectly made up in my mind.

Letting go meant I got to hold on tighter to me, the me that
deserves better, the me that will give that love to someone that will
care for it ever so softly.

allow me to reintroduce myself

You'll never be the same person you were a year ago. Maybe not even the same person you were a month ago or a week ago. We're constantly evolving.

Evolution happens gradually; we're all doing that without trying. We adapt and evolve all the time. However, I think it takes intention to change, to be a new version of you. Change is an act of becoming. Change is a decision *you* make to be someone you love. Someone you care about. You have to decide who it is that you want to become because without clarity, without a gentle push from yourself, the universe will force something else upon you that you may or may not like. Appreciate this version of you because there is so much uncovered depth to who you are. Think about that 'best self' version of yourself that you'd like to introduce yourself as.

After all we've been through together in this book, I'd like to reintroduce myself because I think as you can tell a lot has happened. I've made a lot of decisions. I've evolved a lot, and I've welcomed a whole lot of change. Sure, my name hasn't changed. Outside looking in, I am the same Alexa Glazer. However, I feel quite different. On a spirit and soul level, I am quite different. My insides have been so deeply rearranged. I no longer feel broken like I have so many times in the past.

I no longer feel like I am too much or not enough even though that was my mantra for years. Sometimes I can't help but wonder if people love, like, or hate this new version of me, but to be honest, I don't totally care. I love this version of me so fiercely that if anyone else doesn't, I am simply not for them. I am simply not their people, and they are not mine. That's okay.

This can get confusing because as you change, shift, and mold yourself into the person you're about to reintroduce yourself as, you might feel like you have contradictory voices on your shoulders constantly bickering about things like thoughts, ideas, and feelings. That at all times you have a clear view of the old you who wants to remind you about all that is your past. Your patterns, your mistakes, your habits. Then, you see the current you who is really just trying their best to stay afloat. Finally, you can so clearly see the vision of you at your highest freaking self. That vision of you is clear from the grace, change, and energy you've been tirelessly working toward. Have you ever felt this way? It can get complicated when you're not paying close enough attention to the details revolving around your space.

All of a sudden you feel somewhere foreign, blasted into another planet of sorts. You're not sure how to act, what to say, where to go, or how to feel. It's as if the only thing you can do for a while is sit and observe. To take in all that is around you. So, here I am completely blasted into what feels like another universe. The universe that is the in-between we've been talking about. Technically I'm still on this planet, still in Ohio, but not able to totally and completely understand what happens here. It's taken me a long time to feel safe, but now that I do, I never want to leave.

I've had to try really hard to honor this new version of who I am because at times it felt like too much. This version feels so different that there have been moments when I don't even recognize myself in the mirror. Not because minor things about my body have changed, or my style has shifted, or my hair is dark again, but because on a soul level, I am beaming. My heart feels rearranged, my mind feels expansive, my insides feel slightly unknown. There is always a lot to discover. Yes, on the outside I look like Alexa freaking Glazer. The one you know (and hopefully love). However, I can't deny what's happened and continues to happen daily. This can feel lonely, and it can feel quite strange at first, but if any of this is resonating with your heart, I hope you can find it somewhere inside of you to keep going just like I am.

Reintroducing yourself can be so exciting. It is for me, and I think it's important to reintroduce yourself into new seasons of life. With each reintroduction, you get to acknowledge that you are one step closer to being the person you not only wanted to become but were brave enough to actually become.

As you change, your awareness comes in what I feel are slightly cringey moments. Moments where you learn about yourself and have to decide, "Is this something I want to keep about myself or is it time to retire that version of me?" The first couple times you start to feel and see this awareness, you try to avoid it. At least I did. It's icky, and it makes you raw to your core. Your body wants to protect you and keep you safe, and trust me, I understand completely. It's hard to feel safe in this unknown space, especially when you learn about the things you subconsciously have done for far too long. However, as you get closer, you start to feel safer than you ever have. It might even be the first time you've ever felt safe at all.

At the beginning of this change, you may start to question yourself. I know I did. You feel the weight of the paradox "I've always been this person" with "I'm so different from who I was." Not everyone is going to like this, and you're going to leave some people behind. The only thing that matters is that *you* like or dislike you.

Now, of course I don't want you to dislike yourself. What I mean by this is you get to be the judge. Please pay attention to who appreciates each version of who you are. Those are your people. Please pay attention to who you are happy and grateful to introduce this version of yourself to.

Rarely are people's motives unselfish. Meaning there are definitely people in my life who don't like this new version of me because the old version of Alexa gave them what they wanted, not what she wanted (or needed). Which means, if there's a dramatic change within you, some people simply aren't going to like it. The real breakthrough comes when you just don't care anymore. It comes when you're okay knowing that some people are going to drop off from your life and only come back when they hope you'll once again give them what they need. Remember you're now stronger than that. Rather than create a future that solely revolves around what others need, focus on creating a future that revolves around what you need.

WHO AM I?

Lately, I feel like I need a damn name tag that says, "Hey, I'm Alexa. If we've met before, you probably won't remember me. I am a recovering people pleaser, someone working on having and maintaining boundaries, and someone who knows what she wants and isn't going to settle for anything less." Sure, this all sounds great. It sounds like I have it all together. Wrong. This new name tag feels uncomfortable to wear. Kinda like when you have a tag on a shirt that you have to cut off because it's so itchy.

If we break down this new name tag of mine, I look at the girl who was a people pleaser. I felt like my mission was to serve people, which meant that in order to serve, I had to say yes to everything. To constantly put others before myself. To know deep down that I wanted to say no but would say yes instead. Eventually putting everyone else first made me burn out (this feeling royally sucks). It made me miss me. It made making decisions for myself really difficult because I wasn't used to it. I didn't know how to do it. When I did start to make these hard decisions for myself, I realized those people I said yes to before didn't like the change in me because they now were being told no (which is a complete sentence, just so you know). Overall, some people didn't like it, and that meant that they would have to do things for themselves now.

Then there were the boundaries, or lack thereof. This goes hand in hand with pleasing people. Even if I was sleep deprived, lying in bed with the lights off, ready to go to bed, and my phone rang from a friend that needed to vent or talk about something they were going through, I would answer their call over sleeping. Or the amount of times a client of mine would miss a deadline and I would graciously do it after the fact instead of doing something else I was currently working on. Or not wanting to leave my house and someone asking to hang out and I would choose them over me because I didn't want to hurt their feelings. Even when I didn't want to, I said yes to everything, and I was constantly going above and beyond.

If you would have asked me what a boundary was two years ago, I had no clue what that remotely meant, and I'm being totally serious. When I was living in the van, I made a friend named Jillie. She was a life coach and my type of people. We were recording a podcast episode, and boundaries came up during our conversation. After we stopped recording the episode, I was intrigued. I wanted to know more about boundaries and what her specific boundaries were. I truly felt like my mind was blown because for me, boundaries didn't exist. At this point, I couldn't have ever imagined saying no to anything. It seems so silly, but I know a lot of you are feeling this right now.

Then, there was me settling, especially me settling in my relationships. You probably made that assumption for yourself as we went through the boyfriends and "situations" I've been in. I didn't ask (nor expect) people to return a similar type of love, effort, or care. I just thought this was me—the giver. At the time, I didn't think I was settling, and I definitely didn't do it on purpose, but it's still a pattern of my past. One I had to work the most on in this healing journey of mine. I would say this is the area where I have the most baggage. No one wants to believe they're settling, but I was, and I can see that clearly now.

We all want to feel loved, to be validated by someone who cares about us. Sometimes we want it so badly that we settle. We think that our standards must be too high, that the someone we write about in our journals doesn't actually exist, that it's impossible to find someone who will actually treat us the way we want *and should* be treated. Decide right now, with me, to no longer accept the bare minimum. To no longer accept the shit you know isn't acceptable behavior. I pinky promise to do the same.

All this to say, I don't have it all figured out. Change is scary, but so is staying the same. Don't you agree? I don't know what I'm doing the majority of the time (no one does). This work we decide to do for ourselves isn't pretty; it's quite fuzzy. I've been busy doing this work. Trying to trust myself in the process. Trying to love myself fiercely in this process. So I sit here, deeply in this process of reintroducing myself, and I promise you, it's worth it. People are going to love this new version of you, and most importantly, you'll love this new version of yourself, too.

IT'S ABOUT BALANCE

Think back to when you were on the playground in elementary school and you were trying to get across a balance beam. There are a few different scenarios that may have happened. You could try and then fall off the beam, which could potentially leave you getting hurt or be temporarily embarrassed about people seeing you fall. You could be too scared to try at all because you don't want to fall, get hurt, or be embarrassed, and you'd always wonder what it would feel like to actually get across. You could also try over and over and over again to make your way across the beam as it swayed back and forth, sometimes falling and trying again, sometimes making it across more effortlessly, but being really proud of yourself for doing it regardless of the outcome.

Does any of this sound familiar? When you're trying to be a better version of yourself, it feels a lot like this. It's scary and possibly feels risky, but that's what fear tries to do. It paralyzes us and tries to stop us from trying new things. It focuses our mind on what would happen if we fell rather than what would happen if we made it across.

The difference between those that can and can't make it across the balance beam (no matter what age) is the trust they have within themselves to get there. It's the patience they have for the length of time it may take them. It's the kindness they have for themselves when they sway, slip, or maybe even fall. It all goes back to trust.

I think walking across a balance beam is a lot like healing, it's a lot like grieving, a lot like loving. We constantly sway back and forth if we allow ourselves to. Only those willing to trust, have patience, and be kind are the ones that continue to practice regardless of how long it takes and the number of times they fall. Truth is, as cliche as it may be, every time we fall, we always have the opportunity to get back up.

I feel like I finally made it over a very long (miles long) balance beam. I have fallen off, gotten hurt, and been embarrassed along the way. I've had to take breaks, start over, and completely walk away at times. When I finally decided to trust, have patience, and be a little kinder to myself along the way, I made it. Sure, there were some bumps and bruises, but nothing I couldn't handle. Nothing you can't handle, either.

Now that I'm over here, I find myself a bit flustered and maybe even a little discombobulated. I constantly am asking myself, "Is this what a healthy version of Alexa looks like, feels like, and sounds like? Is this me at my highest self? Is this the best version of who I am?" These questions feel big and the answer feels even bigger. The answer is yes, you are the healthiest, best, most badass, highest version of you right now. Although I sometimes still flounder, I'm now aware enough to know how to fix it or be in it.

I know this may sound silly because I didn't actually walk across any sort of balance beam, but the act of trying to get where I am today definitely feels like it. That balance beam has looked like me going to therapy every single week. It's been me writing down my thoughts and feelings almost daily. It's been my relationships, both good and bad. It's been creating those boundaries, lots of crying, questioning myself, and everything *in-between*. With each and every step, I have certainly swayed.

This new version of me still exists in her same physical space, which to be honest, is also new for me. I always thought that if I didn't feel good in an environment, I had to leave. This proves that you can feel "good" no matter what if you help yourself feel that. This new Alexa (the one now writing this) still goes to the same coffee shops, drinks her favorite beer, and reads every book she can get her hands on. She also still hates doing her laundry, grocery shopping, and is working on breaking bad habits. She still has trouble maintaining boundaries but tries a lot harder to honor them. She still wants to find her person. She's just no longer settling for one, and she is as clear as a blue sky on a Las Vegas summer about what she wants in that man. She still pleases people every now and again, but she tries her hardest not to. Things just feel different.

I eventually made it across the miles of balance beam because I decided to keep practicing. To keep acknowledging that the only way to get better at something was to do it over and over and over again. To *choose* doing those things over and over and over again. I realized that nothing is a quick fix and that if this is something I truly wanted, that I had to make even the hard stuff (like going to therapy weekly) part of my self-care routine. These things became non-negotiables even when I felt too tired to go. I wanted to feel alive, and part of feeling alive was deciding to keep doing the hard shit.

The thing I quickly realized is that even when you break through to this version of you that you want to be, some things still stay the same. You don't make it across, snap your fingers, and never cry a tear again. I don't even think that would be nice, actually. Things still aren't going to go according to plan. Things are still going to go "wrong." The difference is that you're okay with it. You have found the peace you've been unknowingly searching for. It's been there all along; you just hadn't grabbed it yet. You now handle things with grace and you keep going even though you're swaying back and forth.

For instance, when things went wrong or not according to my plan, my reaction to things started to change. In fact, there now isn't much of a reaction at all, or at least not some long, drawn-out one like in the past. I leave space to have a reaction, and I acknowledge that reaction, but I don't fixate on it like I did in the past. The fixation and festering is what used to make me question myself and my worth. I'm now proud of myself and my worth. I don't need to let my reactions—to things I couldn't control anyway—make me question myself again. Walking on a balance beam through life has allowed me to push the limits of my mind and my heart a little more. To be okay with the swaying, the falling, the pausing.

I don't know how often you think about the older versions of yourself. The one on the other side of the balance beam. The one that wished for the things you're doing now. The difficult part in doing this is not comparing yourself to who you used to be. I do this a lot and wish I didn't.

If I think about Alexa a year ago, wow, my heart goes out to her. Sure, I look in the mirror and I physically see the same person, with the same birthmarks, same scars, and same overall frame, but I also look in the mirror and sometimes I don't see anything I used to see. Because the Alexa a year ago looked in the mirror and wasn't kind to herself. This new Alexa, though, is so fucking kind. I feel like a brand-new human being. It's like getting introduced to a friend of a friend.

For me personally, I am talking about October 2020 to October 2021—simply twelve months—and what I see in the mirror is wildly different. What I say to myself when I look in the mirror is wildly different. I am thankful for sticking out through this hard season of life. These twelve months were really difficult. Kindness finally caught up to me (thank goodness for that). When I look in the mirror, I see me for who I am and not all of the damaged goods I thought I was before. I see a girl who is no longer empty, drained, and exhausted by another person or by chasing this idea of what I thought life should be. I don't question my every move anymore, I want to get out of bed, and I truly love me.

Can you try looking in the mirror and thinking back to a year ago? Look for how much you've changed and how much you've overcome. Even if you're still smack dab in the middle of that balance beam, acknowledge how far you've come. Think about all of the things you've accomplished, survived, and overcome.

GUT CHECKS AREN'T SO BAD

A lot of times, we think the gut check we get before doing something scary is a bad thing, a warning. It's not always bad, though. It doesn't have to be a warning. Paying attention to your body lets you start understanding how your body talks to you in different ways. Each feeling means something different, but it needs you to pay attention. You have to be brave enough to take that first step toward change, growth, and healing. Look at that gut check as proof that doing something new holds value. Similar to your fears that we talked about earlier, it's telling you that you are interested. It's telling you that it holds value. It's literally making your body react, to feel something deep inside of you.

Think about the last time you fell in love. You got butterflies, right? Let's go back. Imagine yourself on your way to the first date with someone you fell in love with. You questioned all the things you were going to say. You did everything you could to look your best, and the entire time, you just sat looking across at them hoping that you were impressing them as much as they were impressing you. Obviously you went on the date even though you were nervous and questioning it all. You then had that gut check again the first time their lips touched yours, when they asked you to meet their friends and their family, or the first time you were intimate with each other. This gut check was not bad; it was just sending signals to you.

If that doesn't resonate, think back to when you got your driver's license. I don't know about you, but for me, I was *dying* to be able to drive my own car and to not have to wait on my parents to go places or ride my bike miles and miles across town. But when I finally was allowed to drive a car (even with my parents in it), I was fucking terrified. I wondered if I could actually reach the pedals, if I eventually wouldn't have to look in every single mirror at all times to stay straight on the road, or if I would be able to parallel park without hitting a cone. I got butterflies every time I sat in that driver's seat, but I continued to try to learn how to drive and get better because I wanted it that badly.

With each one of these past experiences, your stomach probably dropped, but it wasn't a bad thing, and on top of it, it most likely never even crossed your mind that it was a bad thing. Your body can and will react to things that you want but are still scary. You have to give yourself the opportunity to see what the gut checks mean and to not automatically assume it's something bad. Sit with it, honor it, and maybe try falling in love with yourself so that butterflies don't seem so scary.

BECOMING THE TRUE YOU

I asked you if you ever thought about the older version of yourself. I also want you to get crystal clear on the version of you that you want to be. The version you think your highest self shows up as. What does this person look like? What do they feel consistently? What do they experience on the daily? Where do they live? What do they do? List out in detail all of these tiny moments and begin to realize how important they actually are.

If I close my eyes and think about this version of myself, I imagine me walking out of a house that is hidden away in the mountains but also on a lakeside. It's golden hour in the morning, and I can see the sun between the trees. I'm barefoot, wearing cozy clothes and no make-up, and there's a new book in my hand. I see a supportive person in my life who I am head over heels for. I have a healthy relationship with myself first and them second. I'm intentional about my work and feel connected to my purpose. I am wildly curious about life, love, and everything in-between.

There are more details on exactly how I am living life, what I am doing, and where I am going, but if I take a snapshot of a random morning, that's what I see. I want to challenge you to examine what you see for yourself. To not force something in or out of this picture of what could be.

This is all to say I'm reintroducing myself right now, yes, and I will again and again and again over the years. I am going to be walking from balance beam to balance beam, challenging myself to do the scary things and to constantly have to reintroduce who I am to myself and to the world.

We will forever and always be reintroducing ourselves as someone new, and although that could be scary, it's also exciting as fuck if you let it be. Think about the relationships in your life that no matter how much time has passed, nothing feels different although everything is in fact different. Think about how excited you are to hear about this person's life and the things that have changed in it. Sure, you may be sad you don't get to spend as much time with them. You may grieve the life that you used to get to experience with them, but you're also genuinely so grateful to get the opportunity for them to essentially reintroduce themselves every time y'all finally get to catch up and connect. There are people out there like that for you, too. People that can't wait for you to reintroduce yourself.

Please, get patient, get kind, and trust yourself that you're going to make it across the balance beam. Although I can't do it for you, and this time I can't even hold your hand on the rope with you, I'll be sitting here cheering you on from the sidelines waiting for you to make it across.

February 19, 2020

Your people will love you no matter what. That's why they're your people. They will love you when you are happy and they'll love you when you're sad, angry or inattentive. The people that don't understand these qualities, the people that don't try to understand. They aren't your people. Get close to the ones that want you close and love on them.

March 23, 2020

Not all of us need a quarantine to feel alone. That's something that comes natural to us already. You get it, right? That feeling of sleeping next to someone and feeling lonely. That feeling of having a conversation with someone who's not actually listening. That feeling of disappointment and lack of attention. It doesn't matter if you're in a room full of people or by yourself; it all feels the same. It doesn't matter if you're six feet apart or holding hands; it all feels the same … empty. How is it that sometimes the people that you're closest to don't see you, they don't hear you?

April 30, 2021

I've struggled. I've struggled with loving my body, watching people leave this planet before I thought they "should," my mental health and at times just getting out of bed. I've struggled in my past relationships, setting and holding boundaries, receiving love and feeling anything other than "happy." Needless to say, I'm fucking emotional writing this because I'm about to say something that would have never come out of my mouth before, and if it ever did ... deep down I didn't actually believe it. But here we go ... I fucking love the girl I see in the mirror and in pictures of myself. Truly, unapologetically, whole-freaking-heartedly love her to pieces.

Never have I ever felt like such a badass, felt so beautiful, and like my big ass dreams are as possible as they are, right now. I am Alexa Renee Glazer in all her freaking glory. Wearing her heart proudly on her sleeve and showing each and every struggle to the world in hopes it helps you get through yours, makes you feel less alone, allows you to take that guard down ... even just a bit. If you're struggling too I hope you find a second of peace today. I hope you stand where your feet are and hold on to the hope that every feeling, every emotion, experience, moment is an opportunity to be. To get out of survival mode and into living.

THINGS I'M NO LONGER APOLOGIZING FOR:

Anything I didn't actually do.

Living my life the way that I want to live it.

Not taking someone else's advice.

Saying the word fuck.

Sharing my feelings, even when they're heavy.

Taking up space.

Being happy.

Being sad.

Being anything that makes someone else uncomfortable.

SIGNS YOU'RE TAPPING INTO YOUR TRUE SELF:

You're genuinely proud of yourself for all that you have done to be where you are in this exact moment (aka you're standing taller, feeling better, and putting good out into the world).

You've got an overwhelming giddiness and presence for life (aka you feel alive and at pace with all that the world is).

You care less about logic and more about what feels right to your soul and spirit (aka you're choosing to be more heart-centered).

You focus less on the fear you carry and trust on your intuition (aka you acknowledge and are aware of your feelings and how they show up in your body).

I hope you keep your faith closer to you than your fears. That your courage grows and you keep it close to your heart. I hope you decide to love yourself today. To pop each and every bubble of self-hate, of dismissal, of negative thoughts, and the feelings of being unworthy. That the disgust you've been holding onto for so long starts to disappear. I hope you decide what kind of life you want to live and then say "no" to everything else. You don't have the time to live any other way. I hope you decide to take care of yourself before you try to please someone else. That you form boundaries that no one can break. I hope you ignore the opinions of others that don't suit you. That you know that your opinion is the one that gets the final say. I hope that your heart stretches and you begin to crave the love you give. That love comes to you in the purest of ways. The magic it provides. I hope you decide that the skin you are in is beautiful, it's yours, and it's special. I hope you decide to do the uncomfortable thing for long term comfort you could feel in your own skin. I hope you pick you today and every day. The real you. The one I see, the one I hear. The one worthy of the world. It's your turn.

it's your turn

For a very long time, I thought that I was one of those lucky ones. You know the type of people. The ones that always seem like nothing bad ever happens to them. The people who seemingly (key word seemingly) coast through life without a scar to show off and their entire heart intact. I thought that the stuff you heard about—the bad, the ugly, or even just the lesser of the good—wouldn't happen to me. I was *so* naive. I'm not sure why I felt so privileged other than the fact that … I was. I am. What a gross thing to say out loud and a gross thing to write down for all to see.

From everything you just read, I am now well aware that bad stuff—or the not so fun stuff—happens to all of us at some point. That's something we all have in common actually. We all experience similar things: Relationships ending, broken hearts, people dying, identities shifting. We just experience them at different times, with different magnitudes, attached to different feelings, thoughts, and actions.

I may not believe in the lucky ones anymore, but I do believe that some souls are seen, heard, and loved by the universe differently. I know you agree. That in a world filled with freedom, so many aren't free. Free from their mind, free from others' judgment, free from just being. That their existence is tested daily. This is the part where we can focus on that .01% difference in all of our DNA. Where you can take all that you've learned about your heart, body, and mind and look at the pieces that make you so unique from the rest of us. I've talked about how important it is to connect with others, but please don't forget how important it is to connect with yourself, too.

Maybe your being is and has been craving attention, love, and care. To feel like a somebody, especially when you're feeling like a nobody. To matter to someone, anyone. To be noticed on a deeper level. To be seen for who you are. To be heard for what you stand for. To be known for something special. To be cared for ever so gently. You're not asking for too much, but what is the answer you're giving yourself?

As humans, it's our deepest desire to be seen, heard, known, loved, and cared for. It's also the thing that we deeply fear. This is the thing that made me feel misunderstood in the past. It was something I desired, but I didn't know how to fulfill it. This fear forces us to bury those desires deep down because they feel intangible. Instead, we downplay ourselves and place value in other avenues, and other people, but rarely ourselves. We constantly replay the mantra in our mind, "I'm never enough and always too much." It's time to change that. For you to always feel enough and never too much. This will take time; that's okay. Stay the course.

Lately, this is all I think about. It consumes my heart, my mind, my soul. I think it's easy to assume that it's not what we do that leaves the biggest impact but it's truly how we make people feel. That's the shit that matters. To make people feel seen first, heard second, known in time, loved without the fluff, and cared for with intention. But what do these actually mean?

Being seen isn't just someone looking at you. Being heard isn't just someone listening. Being known isn't them just knowing a minor detail about you. Being loved isn't just saying "I love you," and caring for someone isn't just hugging them when they need it (although it helps). I think this is a timeline of connection and relationships. When we allow ourselves to feel these things for ourselves first and others second, this type of connection is a true game-changer.

It's easy for me to tell you how wonderful it is to be seen, but I think most of us don't truly know how to be seen. When this is the case, we're going to continue to deal with the same low standards and shortcomings in our worthiness. We need to be able to put language to our wants, needs, desires, and feelings. If we don't know, no one else can know. The act of seeing, hearing, knowing, loving, and caring for ourselves and others is a practice, one that isn't always graceful or easy.

BEING SEEN

Being seen is feeling noticed and having an undeniable presence with yourself or with someone else. You know when you walk into a room and you can swear that someone looks at you, but you then realize they simply looked past you at someone else? Ugh, this is the worst. This is the opposite of feeling seen and makes us feel a little invisible.

Feeling seen can be anything from someone giving you direct eye contact to truly looking at you—not through you or past you. In order for me to feel seen, I need to feel that the person I am with is showing up in a way that doesn't dismiss me. That they see me by giving me direct eye contact during conversation, maybe acknowledging something I'm wearing, telling me they're proud of something I did, or simply giving me a more than decent hug.

BEING HEARD

Being heard is having your words understood and challenged without another person trying or wanting to change what you're saying. It's knowing that what you have to say matters and is being noted. We've all been in a conversation where you sit there and think, "Did you listen to a word I just said?" Being heard is someone actively listening and not just waiting for the slightest pause to jump in and share their version.

With that being said, being heard can look like having conversation where someone actively listens to everything you have to say without interpreting. This happens to be one of my biggest pet peeves. After listening, they ask follow-up questions that may challenge your thinking but without pushing you to think any other way in that moment.

If I want to be heard, I surround myself with people who will expand my thinking and people who won't give me constant unsolicited advice. I surround myself with people who engage in conversation in a healthy and non-judgmental way.

BEING KNOWN

Feeling known by someone, in my opinion, requires us to feel like we're standing naked in front of someone. I know; this sounds terrifying. I don't mean they're seeing your body, but rather that they're seeing everything that has made you who you are, and they don't run away. In fact, they move closer.

This type of nakedness shows the skeletons in your closet and the baggage you carry. Being this known is having someone be there with you in vulnerability and them loving and liking you anyway. In fact, loving and liking you even more. It's someone seeing a scar and not repeatedly asking where it came from but remembering because you've already told them.

If someone is making me feel known, they're acknowledging emotions I may feel when I'm triggered by an experience. Their awareness is proof that they're remembering something special I shared with them. Feeling known is another person constantly saying, "I want to know even just a little bit more because everything I learn about you becomes important to me."

BEING LOVED

Being loved is all about taking the risk of sharing yourself without the fear—or despite the fear—of being rejected. Being loved outweighs the rest. When you feel loved, it's ultimately about feeling safe and being respected and supported. This may look different for each person, and feeling safe doesn't necessarily mean physically.

I hope that being loved by someone means you feel safe emotionally with them. That you feel safe mentally and intellectually. That being respected isn't just by someone staying faithful to you but being aware of your boundaries, your limits, and your independence.

Last, being supported doesn't mean financially. It means someone being your teammate. Hyping you up when you need it, giving you supportive feedback when you need it, holding you up when you need it. This, to me, is love.

BEING CARED FOR

Last, what does it take for someone to feel truly cared for? It's a state of true acknowledgment outside of a person. The actions of someone who is willing to protect the shit out of you. This person that cares for you is constantly acting from a place of love and empathy.

To me, this type of care is protecting someone for the things you "know" about them. It's no longer just acknowledging that it exists but actually taking action to acknowledge that someone could have been triggered. Chiming in, stepping up, and having someone's back when they feel triggered. You do this as an act of love

LOVE YOURSELF FIRST

My sweet one, the one that doesn't feel loved, that doesn't feel seen, that doesn't feel heard, known, or cared for: You get it. The heartbreak that comes with feeling this way. The smiles that aren't genuine, the constant pit in your gut, the questions you ask about belonging. Lucky ones or not, we all get rocked. I wish I could take your pain away. I wish I could physically give you a piece of my heart. I wish I could hold you, to hug the hate away. I wish I could tell you it's okay. But it's not ... the fight you're fighting is not okay. It's not fair. But you fight anyway. I admire you for it. To continue despite everything. You continue to get back up after every punch. Every gut check. Every reality check.

I'm going to ask you to do something hard. For you to look in the mirror and see, hear, know, love, and care for yourself first. If we don't know how to do this, it's going to be really hard for us to know how someone else can do it for us. This is a battle for a lot of us. We go to war daily with the person that looks back at us in the mirror.

Many of us like to fill that void by finding it elsewhere. To get validation from someone else. Now, the type of love we feel from different people will be just that: different. However it feels really freaking special when you can truly say I love me and I love me hard. Through the good times and the not so good, I love the person I am becoming. To look in the mirror and see a dark spot and not hate it. To have an opinion about something and know that you're allowed to have one. To know that this experience you went through is not something to hide. To respect, support, and make yourself feel safe in your body and in your mind. And of course to care for yourself by standing up for who you are because you're worth that.

As you figure out how exactly your soul needs to feel these things I'll sit for you, I'll listen to you, I'll open my heart for you, and I've got your back.

TO THE PERSON HEALING RIGHT NOW:

You're in it. Deeply in this process. You're thinking to yourself, "What in the actual fuck is happening and when the fuck is this going to be over?" You're probably questioning everything and then some.

You're feeling exhausted, alone, and waking up instantly wanting to go back to bed. I wish someone would have warned me that healing is not the euphoric land of unicorns and candy covered streets. That at times, it's dark.

Truth is, we each make a choice to heal or to simply exist. In my opinion, if we are truly living, then we are going to face things that require us to decide if we're going to heal or continue to suffer. What a never-ending cycle

What an epic life you get to experience in all its entirety, so many people don't even try. They run from their pain, but you're choosing peace. So friend, it may not be glamorous. It may feel like we never fully heal, but what I do know is that we somehow stop letting these events, triggers, and moments have the control. That we're able to tell them kindly to shut the fuck up.

It's your turn to gain the power back. I know you were hoping for butterflies and rainbows and got anything but that, but please know you're doing a damn good job right now. I see it; you'll feel it soon.

IN CASE YOU FORGOT OR SOMEONE TOLD YOU OTHERWISE:

You are human.

Your feelings are valid.

You're supposed to feel things.

Sometimes it feels good.

Sometimes it doesn't feel very good.

It's all necessary.

It's all going to be okay.

WHAT IT MEANS TO BE HUMAN:

You learn *self-acceptance*.

You realize this is done through forgiveness and letting go.

You're deeply patient with yourself.

You begin to love every inch of your being. Your body, your heart, your mind.

You learn *presence*.

You allow the *pursuit* of peace to take force and you become "okay" with the feelings, thoughts, and experiences that you can't control.

You *play*. You find that childhood wonder you may have lost along the way.

You become *radically resilient*. The skeleton key to being human and being truly alive.

I mean it, it's your turn

I got to this last page and had no idea what to say to you. I felt blank and numb. I wrote and deleted this paragraph a million times over. I felt like I didn't have the words to finish this book with a bang. To finish it with words that would move you to tears, inspire you to change your life, move you to feel something. I had a bit of an identity crisis if we're being honest. The impostor syndrome set in, the old versions of me antagonized, and I was ready to go into full self-sabotage mode.

I sat here wondering if I accomplished what I promised you, if there was any point to this book. But as I re-read these sentences, stories, and chapters over and over and over again, I realized that getting to this last page meant that I was just sentences away from letting go of the old narratives of myself—the old versions of who I was—for good, and any resentment and shame that came along with them. Amen!

But I also started to wonder if I was actually safe enough in my body to do so, and I began to mourn those old versions of myself. I don't think I've ever consciously done that before, but it's powerful.

At the beginning of this book, I gave you a permission slip. That slip told you to claim yourself, to change your mind, and to feel all that is the human experience. Now, here we are. We are deep in the dark basements of our hearts. I hope you've been able to trust yourself and love on the person you are today because right now, I'm giving you permission to let that old person go. To gratefully say goodbye. To have a beautiful fucking funeral for the version of you that's no longer here.

If I learned anything in writing this book (and there's been a lot), it's knowing you can change as much of yourself as you want to, but if you don't forgive and let go of that old version, it's still going to control the new you indirectly. So we're going to do it together. We're going to gracefully let go.

Most importantly, you're not alone and you matter. That's why we're doing this work. In this time we spent together, I truly hope you've honored that your standards are not too high, your dreams are not too big, that you can trust your intuition fully, and that you never feel like you have to do anything alone. That you know that you are not defined by any one event or experience in your life. That together we are here in the pursuit of peace, and please, find it in you to welcome your feelings even when you fear them.

You are seen, heard, known, loved, and cared for. My hope is that right now, you feel alive.

My whole freaking heart,

Lex

acknowledgements

Jonathan, thank you from the bottom of my heart for helping me believe that my sadness reminds me that I am alive.

Hannah, my beautiful editor, thank you for challenging me in the softest way and guiding me to creating a book that I am so proud of.

Mom, Nikki, and Mindy, thank you for being my safe place to land and loving me unconditionally.

My forever humans and favorite people (you know who you are), thank you for being you. I am so grateful to have such warm, kind-hearted, and loving people in my life.

Readers, thank you for holding this book in your hands and so gently to your heart. My hope was to tug at your heart strings, but instead, you're tugging at mine.

about the author

Alexa Glazer is a speaker, author, and leader. She guides humans to **radical resilience** through *self-acceptance, presence, and play*. She uses her words, both written and spoken to honestly and openly connect with you, your heart, and your greatest desires.

She is the author of the book you're holding in your hands, *Your Permission Slip*, as well as her first book *Livin' the dream today because tomorrow is not promised*. She is also the co-host to her podcast Chasing Alignment.

Alexa is Cleveland made but adventure grown. A full-time feeler, powered by love and hugs. A grief advocate and the stranger who will be your best friend in 30 seconds. She's on the pursuit of peace and never plays it small. Her superpower is how much she believes in people and endless possibilities. She's not perfect and she doesn't want to be. Alexa is so glad you're here!

You can follow Alexa on Instagram @alexaglazer_ or find out more on www.alexaglazer.com

CPSIA information can be obtained
at www.ICGtesting.com
Printed in the USA
JSHW050005200922
30723JS00004B/22